LATIN AMERICAN TRAVEL

Travels in Brazil

BY HENRY KOSTER

Edited and with an Introduction
by C. Harvey Gardiner

SOUTHERN ILLINOIS UNIVERSITY PRESS

Carbondale and Edwardsville

Contents

Introduction

In the opening decades of the nineteenth century, Brazil was a land of change, much of which transformation was stimulated by foreign travelers. The trip forced upon the Portuguese Court when onrushing hordes of Napoleonic soldiers dictated its swift removal from Lisbon to Brazil was quite possibly the most significant single factor. Beginning in 1808, a succession of decrees by João, the Prince Regent, not only liberalized Brazilian life in its economic and cultural realms, they also paved the way for those foreign contacts which included the wide-eyed traveler with pen in hand.

The first of the literate English travelers in this period, Thomas Lindley, master of a trading vessel, reached Brazil in 1802. Then the Portuguese colony was wallowing in a maze of restrictions aimed at maintaining the ancient mercantilist doctrine of mother-country supremacy. Lindley's goods were declared contraband; and the unwanted Englishman became a prisoner of the authorities. At best, Lindley's acquaintance with Brazil was limited to the port communities of Pôrto Seguro and Baía. His *Narrative of a Voyage to Brasil* (London, 1805)—with a German edition in 1806 and another English one in 1808—is essentially an account of his treatment as a prisoner in 1802-3, not an assessment of Brazilian life in any extended dimension.

Another Englishman, John Mawe, was in South America when Napoleon's machinations in the Iberian Peninsula landed João and the Court on the beach at Rio de Janeiro. By way of the Plata region, where Mawe and the ship and goods related to the commercial experiment to which he was a party fell into the hands of Spanish authorities—and he spent time in prison—the author of *The Mineralogy of Derbyshire* went to Rio de Janeiro. En route

he briefly glimpsed the island of Santa Catarina, Santos
and São Paulo. Royal permission allowed him, the first
foreigner so honored, to visit the gold and diamond min-
ing district, especially in the neighborhoods of Villa Rica
(Ouro Prêto) and Tejuco (Diamantina). Early in 1810,
after a stay of not quite two and one-half years in Brazil,
Mawe returned to England. There, in London, his *Travels
in the Interior of Brazil* was published in 1812.

Before Mawe had departed from Brazil, Henry Koster, the author of the present work, had arrived there. His
childhood in Lisbon, where the family had commercial interests, had afforded him more than a command of the
Portuguese language. "England is my country, but my
native soil is Portugal," he wrote years later; "I belong to
both, and whether in the company of Englishmen, of
Portuguese, or of Brazilians, I feel equally among my
countrymen." Meanwhile, as the winter of 1809 approached, a frail constitution led Koster to board ship for
Brazil, the military situation in the Iberian Peninsula
precluding a return to Lisbon.

In Recife, where he arrived December 7, 1809, Koster, aided by letters of introduction, soon adjusted himself
to the tempo of Brazilian life. For the next ten months, except for attendance at festivals in Olinda and a Lenten
residence at Poça da Panella, he remained in Recife.

In mid-October, 1810, he left Recife on a northerly
trip which consumed the next four months. By horseback,
he traveled to Goiana, Paraíba, Natal, Açu, Santa Luzia,
Aracati and Fortaleza, then back to Recife. This overland
trek acquainted the eager foreigner with many facts of life
in the *sertão*, including its Indians and those successive
scourges of nature, drought and flood. The hospitality of
strange men and the wonders of even stranger nature Koster regularly recorded in his journal, thereby amassing
materials which later added color and fresh detail to his
account of a region about which Englishmen would read
for the first time.

"Eight days after my return from Ceará," Koster

wrote, "arrived a vessel from England, bringing letters which obliged me to leave Pernambuco and proceed to Maranhão. As a cargo could not be obtained for the brig at the former place, the consignee determined to send her to Maranhão, and being myself desirous of taking advantage of the first opportunity, I prepared for the voyage, and sailed in the course of forty-eight hours."

The urgency with which Koster thus identified himself with Anglo-Brazilian commerce invites speculation. In the course of his two-volume work about Brazil, from which one gains and retains the impression that Koster was a gentleman of leisure, an expatriate seeking restoration of health, one seldom encounters economic motivation for his activities in Brazil. Yet in February, 1811, after a long and fatiguing journey, during which he had suffered a serious attack of ague, Koster hastily forsook the comforts of Recife in pursuit of English commercial advantage at Maranhão. Between the lines one concludes that Koster could not and did not renounce his commercial heritage, and that he, conscious of good story-line, intentionally left untold that side of his Brazilian experience.

After six weeks in Maranhão and environs, where he found a despotic governor who was in marked contrast to the genial governor of Pernambuco, Koster sailed to England. Of the interval between his arrival in Falmouth on May 20, and his departure from Portsmouth on November 20, 1811—in time to avoid the rigors of the English winter—we know scarcely anything.

Returned to Recife in the Christmas season of 1811, Koster soon set out with a *capitão-mor* as that officer toured his jurisdiction and inspected his men. This journey took the Englishman to Olinda, Paulista, Bom Jardim, Limoeiro and other places in which he broadened his awareness of Brazil, especially its hospitality, economic life and military organization. Shortly after his return to Recife, Koster negotiated a lease on a nearby sugar plantation.

Except for brief visits in Goiana and Monteiro, Kos-

ter spent the interval between early April, 1812 and early
December, 1813 at Jaguaribe plantation. There, a friendly neighbor of priest and plantation owner and a kindly
master of both free and slave labor, he savored and specu-
lated about multiple aspects of Brazilian life. Perhaps,
too, the illnesses—somewhat vaguely referred to simply
as ague—that plagued him both in the summer of 1812
and the spring of 1813 encouraged his capacity for both
reflection and narration.

In December, 1813, Koster turned his back on Jaguaribe as he moved to the island of Itamaracá and undertook
the management of a second sugar plantation. Aside from
a trip to Pilar with a clergyman, a canoe trip to Igaraçu,
and visits to Agua Fria plantation and Recife, Koster
spent his remaining time in Brazil at this island plantation.
"I received advices from England," he wrote in reference to early 1815, "which rendered necessary my return
home. I gave up my plan of residing in Brazil with reluctance. . . ." Thus closed out a Brazilian residence which,
between late 1809 and early 1815, had acquainted him
intimately with the complexities and both the changing
and changeless aspects of Brazil in that northeastern region which embraced the captaincies of Pernambuco,
Paraíba, Rio Grande do Norte, Ceará and Maranhão.

Armed with his journals and pamphlets by Dr. Man-
uel Arruda da Camara, whom he had sought out in
Goiana in 1810, and a determination to produce a book
about his experiences, Koster speedily set about the completion of that project. To supplement his own awareness
of Brazil, especially in matters of comparative history related to slavery and the slave trade, he turned to Robert
Southey and the famous 14,000-volume library at Keswick
upon which the poet laureate was basing his own writing
on Brazil. The poet laureate and the traveler were not
strangers.

When Southey and Koster first met is not known.
Perhaps they were acquainted before Henry's initial departure for Brazil—after all, during the thirty years in

Portugal that saw the reverend Herbert Hill amassing the library which he put at the disposal of nephew Robert Southey, he quite likely had crossed the paths of the Kosters. Southey's own travels in Portugal might have led to his meeting the Koster family. Even if Southey and Koster were not personally acquainted before 1809, it is quite possible that they met in 1811 during Koster's brief return to his homeland. Perhaps the man in uncertain health spent a summer holiday in the Lake District at Keswick on Derwent Water. By that time Southey had published the first volume of his *History of Brazil* (1810) and could use the on-the-spot assistance of a smart Englishman soon to return to South America. Eventually, in his third volume, Southey's acknowledgments came to include "Henry Koster, for various communications from Pernambuco, and especially for a Narrative of the Insurrection in that Captaincy, in 1710–11, transcribed from the original manuscript. . . ." Henry had helped Robert and in time the latter reciprocated handsomely.

When the first edition of Koster's *Travels in Brazil*, a hefty quarto, appeared in October, 1816, it was dedicated to Robert Southey "in memorial of affectionate respect and gratitude." In the preface, Koster elaborated, "I have had the advantage of Mr. Southey's advice and extensive library."

So it was that Henry Koster studied and wrote at Greta Hall in Keswick, doing both with the exacting dedication that enabled him to ready his manuscript for publication in less than one year. From Southey's shelves he took down such French sources as Pierre Barrère's *Nouvelle relation de la France équinoxiale*, Jean Baptiste Dutertre's *Histoire général des Antilles*, and Jean Baptiste Labat's two works, *Nouveau voyage aux isles de l'Amérique* and *Voyage du chevalier Des Marchais . . . à Cayenne;* such English works as Henry Bolingbroke's *A Voyage to the Demerary*, Thomas Clarkson's works on the slave trade, Bryan Edwards' *The History, Civil and Commercial, of the British West Indies*, Richard Ligon's *A True and Exact History of the Island of Barbados*,

C. W. Pasley's *Essay on the Military Policy and Institutions of the British Empire*, Dr. George Pinckard's *Notes on the West Indies* and the first volume of Southey's own *History of Brazil*. Among the Portuguese-language materials used by Koster, in addition to Dr. Arruda da Camara's dissertation on the plants of Brazil and his essay on the utility of establishing gardens in Brazil, were two journals, *Correio Braziliense* and *Investigador Portuguez*.

Many books enriched the comparative historical sections of his work on plantation agriculture, slavery and the slave trade, wherein he held up French and English New World experience alongside that of Brazil. Such themes, of course, were tangential to Koster's personal observations. His own experience, however, was amplified occasionally by appeals to history. In so doing, he cited Southey a score of times.

Travels in Brazil was initially published in London by Longman, Hurst, Rees, Orme, and Brown, the house which had published the first volume of Southey's *History of Brazil* and would publish the remaining volumes by 1819. One might conclude that Southey helped Koster to a publisher and indeed he might have done so. However, it should be noted that Longman, Hurst, Rees, Orme, and Brown, for reasons that are not readily apparent today, was then much interested in Brazil. Four years before handling Koster's manuscript, the same publishers had produced Mawe's *Travels in the Interior of Brazil*. Southey, meanwhile, kept at his *History of Brazil* and before completion, on June 23, 1819, many of his pages sparkled with references to Koster's book.

Henry Koster's life, made memorable by his one book, was a short one. Luiz da Camara Cascudo, who translated the work in 1941 for his fellow Brazilians under the title *Viagens ao Nordeste do Brasil*, asserts that Koster returned to Pernambuco in the autumn of 1816, witnessed the revolution in Recife on March 6, 1817, and died in his adopted transatlantic homeland, possibly early in 1820, age unknown, but young in heart.

Travels in Brazil, on the other hand, has proved to be ageless. Southey, a power in certain English critical circles, penned the anonymous 44-page review of Koster's work which appeared in the January, 1817 issue of the *Quarterly Review*. Although chiefly a narrative summary garnished with numerous direct quotations, the review contributed to the widespread acceptance which the book speedily won. Southey praised Koster's "perfect knowledge of the language," "his feelings and principles. . . ." "The general spirit of the book, indeed, is excellent," Southey insisted, "presenting a faithful picture of a very interesting stage in the progress of society." Other reviewers were equally generous with their praise.

The one-volume quarto edition of 1816 was quickly followed, in October, 1817, by a two-volume octavo edition by the original publisher. That same year a similar edition emerged in Philadelphia, from the presses of M. Carey and Son. The title that crossed the Atlantic to the United States also crossed the channel to Germany that year, a one-volume German edition being published in Weimar.

The following year, 1818, Jay's French translation appeared in Paris in two volumes. A second German translation was published in Leipzig in 1831 and a second printing of Jay's translation emerged in Paris in 1846.

In 1869, full sixty years after Koster's initial entry into Brazil, his countryman Captain Richard F. Burton published his *Explorations of the Highlands of the Brazil*. In his opening pages, before turning to his own travels down the São Francisco River, Burton assessed the already voluminous travel literature about Brazil. For some of the Portuguese, English, American, French, Dutch and other authors there was no note of evaluation, but for one, "the accurate Koster," there was high praise in a single word.

Travels in Brazil has been twice translated in Brazil, by Antonio C. de A. Pimentel, who unfortunately worked from a French text at turn of century, and recently (1941) by the able Luiz da Camara Cascudo. Readers of English, meanwhile, have been limited to the editions of 1816 and 1817, the latter of which has served as the basis of the present edition.

In the century and a half since the initial publication of Koster's book, Brazil has been the subject of hundreds of travel accounts, many of them by specialists—anthropologists, astronomers, artists, botanists, engineers, entomologists, hunters, ichthyologists, mathematicians, mineralogists, missionaries, naturalists, naval officers, and ornithologists, to categorize but a few. All, for their own reporting, might well have looked to Koster's standards of accuracy and breadth and depth.

Travels in Brazil is a remarkably full and balanced account of one significant region of that mammoth land. Either Koster had read widely and had become aware of the ingredients of good writing through dint of hard effort or he was intuitively a story-teller, a man who easily and naturally wove the commonplace as well as the unique of everyday experience into the fabric of words which fairly mirrored the realities of life. Without abusing truth, his narrative is picturesque and anecdotal. It often exhibits an almost casual conversational tone.

Koster's interest in Brazilian manners and customs was unceasing: dances and dinners, festivals and funerals, weddings and work patterns, christenings and conversations, houses and hospitality—all these and more repeatedly drew the attention that blended curiosity and objectivity about Brazilian life from the level of governors and bishops to slaves and wild Indians.

Whereas most travelers, by virtue of their professional interests, economic pursuits or linguistic limitations, develop limited capacities for reporting, Henry Koster had every advantage on his side. He had no narrow, limiting reason for being in Brazil, indeed he had no compelling economic demands upon his time and outlook. His leisure, combined with mastery of the language from the moment he set foot on Brazilian soil, gave him seldom-paralleled advantages. Prior travel in Portugal, France and Flanders afforded him a basis for comparative reaction to things and circumstances outside the norms of English life.

He enjoyed blazing a trail, so to speak, as the first Englishman to describe the *sertão*. At the samet ime, his sense of decency led him to advocate clothing above the waist for all slaves. And possibly more than a little of his national nature shone through as he stated his conviction that British merchants were invigorating the tastes and the economy of Brazil.

Even as he generally advocated evolutionary change in Brazil, he was instantaneous and unceasing in his condemnation of slavery, the slave trade and those "useless beings," the friars of northeastern Brazil. Time and time again he exhibited a total lack of color prejudice. What he liked, he liked as an honest man; what he disliked, he disliked as an honest man.

The editorial method which presents a work within less than one-half its original size, and yet retains the author's own words, requires a word of explanation. The abridgment has followed these lines: a) chapters based on historical research rather than personal observation, e.g. those concerning the slave trade and treaty relations between England and Portugal, have been deleted; b) the lengthy appendix, wherein Koster atones for being neither botanist nor zoologist by offering derived scientific data, is also deleted; c) the appeals to history, in support of the author's own experience, are much reduced if not eliminated, as too is the hearsay; d) some anecdotes are retained for their folkloric flavor but most are deleted as repetitious reinforcements of the author's own experiences; e) all footnotes, bibliographical and expository, have been omitted; and f) the preface, dedication, map and illustrations have been deleted.

The wordy chapter headings have been simplified; and similarly the table of contents has been condensed. Occasional chapters, because of unity of subject-matter—e.g. the overland trip of 1810–11, various aspects of agricultural life, and the free and slave population—have been consolidated.

An occasional word, e.g. segar, has been modernized. English spellings, e.g. centre, labour, have been converted to the American forms. Koster's employment of foreign words, informative and colorful rather than pedantic or irritating, is honored and retained, the only changes being those that bring his Portuguese into line with modern Brazilian practice. Slight modifications occasionally attend capitalization and punctuation.

C. HARVEY GARDINER

October 1, 1965

Travels in Brazil

First Impressions
at Recife

If my health had not required a change of climate, I should not perhaps so soon have accomplished the wish I had often expressed of leaving England for a short time. An immediate removal was judged expedient; and as the ports of Spain and Portugal were either closed to British subjects, or at least not in a state to be visited by an invalid, I determined upon Brazil; to which my friends agreed. I fixed upon Pernambuco, because a gentleman, who had for many years been acquainted with my family, was about to embark for that place, and from the favorable reports of the people and climate which I had received from several persons. On the 2d November 1809, I set sail from Liverpool in the ship "Lucy."

We had a very prosperous passage of thirty-five days, without any occurrence worthy of particular notice. We distinguished the hill upon which stands the city of Olinda, a little to the northward; and some leagues to the southward, Cape Santo Agostinho; a nearer view discovered to us the town of Santo Antonio do Recife, almost ahead with the shipping in front of it; the dreary land between it and Olinda, which is one league distant, and coconut groves northward, as far as the eye can reach; southward of the town are also seen great numbers of coconut trees, woods, and scattered cottages. The situation of Olinda is the highest in the neighborhood.

Nothing this day created so much astonishment on board our ship, amongst those who had not been before upon this coast, as the *Jangadas*, sailing about in all directions. These are simply rafts of six logs, of a peculiar species of light timber, lashed or pinned together; a large latine sail; a paddle used as a rudder; a sliding keel let down between the two center logs; a seat for the steersman, and

a long forked pole, upon which is hung the vessel containing water, the provisions, etc. These rude floats have a
most singular appearance at sea, no hull being apparent
even when near them. They are usually managed by two
men, and go closer to the wind than any description of
vessel.

A large rowboat at last made its appearance, dou-
bling the end of the reef near the small fort, which was
declared to be that which brings off the pilots. The *patrão-
mor*, harbor master, in his naval uniform, likewise came on
board. A large launch followed the pilot, manned chiefly
by Negroes, almost naked: the color of these men, the
state in which they were, their noise and bustle, when
certainly there was no occasion for it, and their awkwardness, were to me all new. This very first communication
with the shore gave me an idea, for the moment, that the
manners of the country at which I had arrived, were still
more strange than they actually proved to be.

We left the ship and proceeded to the shore. Here was
a new scene indeed. We had taken the letter bag with us;
the crowd of well-dressed persons upon the quay was
great; they saw the bag, and soon their anxiety for news
overcame their politeness; the letters were asked for, and
at last we gave them up, and they were scrambled for,
each man seeking his own. We had landed at the customhouse wharf upon a busy day, and the Negroes too were
all clamor and bustle. Their hideous noise when carrying
any load, bawling out some ditty of their own language,
or some distich of vulgar Portuguese rhyme; the numerous
questions asked by many persons who met us, and the very
circumstance of seeing a population consisting chiefly of
individuals of a dark color, added to the sound of a new
language, with which, although I was acquainted, still I
had not since very early youth been in a country where it
was generally spoken; all combined to perplex and to con-
fuse. I was led along by those who were accustomed to
these scenes, and we proceeded to the house of one of the
first merchants in the place. We were ushered up one pair

of stairs into a room in which were several piles of piece-goods, a table covered with papers, and several chairs. There were four or five persons in the room besides the owner of the house. I delivered my letter of introduction to him and was treated with the greatest civility. Our next visit was to a colonel, who is also a merchant, from whom I met with the same behavior.

As there are no inns or furnished lodgings at Recife, or at Olinda, an acquaintance of my fellow-passenger obtained some temporary rooms for us, and supplied us with what we wanted. We are therefore at last quietly settled in our new habitation, if I may be allowed to call it quiet, while some twenty black women are under the windows bawling out, in almost all tones and keys of which the human voice is capable—oranges, bananas, sweetmeats, and other commodities, for sale.

The town of Santo Antonio do Recife, commonly called Pernambuco, though the latter is properly the name of the captaincy, consists of three compartments, connected by two bridges. The first division of the town is composed of brick houses of three, four, and even five stories in height; most of the streets are narrow, and some of the older houses in the minor streets are of only one story in height, and many of them consist only of the ground floor. The streets of this part, with the exception of one, are paved. In the Square are the customhouse, in one corner, a long, low, and shabby building; the sugar-inspection, which bears the appearance of a dwelling house; a large church, not finished; a coffee house, in which the merchants assemble to transact their commercial affairs; and dwelling houses. There are two churches in use, one of which is built over the stone archway leading from the town to Olinda, at which a lieutenant's guard is stationed. The other church belongs to the priests of the *Congregação da Madre de Deus*. Near to the gateway above-mentioned is a small fort, close to the waterside, which commands it. To the northward is the residence of the Port-Admiral, with the government timberyards attached to it: these are small, and the work going on in them is very trifling. The cotton market, warehouses, and presses, are also in this part of the town.

The bridge which leads to Santo Antonio has an archway at either end, with a small chapel built upon each; and at the northern arch is stationed a sergeant's guard of six or eight men. The bridge is formed in part of stone arches, and in part of wood: it is quite flat, and lined with small shops, which render it so narrow that two carriages cannot pass each other upon it.

Santo Antonio, or the middle town is composed chiefly of large houses and broad streets; and if these buildings had about them any beauty, there would exist here a certain degree of grandeur: but they are too lofty for their breadth, and the ground floors are appropriated to shops, warehouses, stables, and other purposes of a like nature. The shops are without windows, and the only light they have is admitted from the door. There exists as yet very little distinction of trades; thus all descriptions of manufactured goods are sold by the same person. Some of the minor streets consist of low and shabby houses. Here are the Governor's palace, which was in other times the Jesuits' convent; the treasury; the town hall and prison; the barracks, which are very bad; the Franciscan, Carmelite, and Penha convents, and several churches, the interiors of which are very handsomely ornamented, but very little plan has been preserved in the architecture of the buildings themselves. It comprises several squares, and has, to a certain degree, a gay and lively appearance. This is the principal division of the town.

The bridge which connects Santo Antonio with Boa Vista is constructed entirely of wood, and has upon it no shops, but is likewise narrow. The principal street of Boa Vista, which was formerly a piece of ground overflowed at high water, is broad and handsome: the rest of this third division consists chiefly of small houses, and as there is plenty of room here, it extends to some distance in a straggling manner. Neither the streets of this part of the

town nor of Santo Antonio are paved. A long embank-
ment has likewise been made, which connects the sand-
bank and town of Santo Antonio with the main land at
Affogados, to the south and west of Boa Vista. The river
Capibaribe, so famous in Pernambucan history, dis-
charges its waters into the channel between Santo Antonio
and Boa Vista, after having run for some distance in a
course nearly east and west.

Some few of the windows of the houses are glazed,
and have iron balconies; but the major part are without
glass, and of these the balconies are enclosed by latticework; and no females are to be seen, excepting the Negro
slaves, which gives a very somber look to the streets. The
Portuguese, the Brazilian, and even the mulatto women,
in the middle ranks of life, do not move out of doors in the
daytime; they hear mass at the churches before daylight,
and do not again stir out, excepting in sedan chairs, or in
the evening on foot, when occasionally a whole family will
sally forth to take a walk.

The three compartments of the town, together, contain about 25,000 inhabitants, or more, and it is increasing
rapidly; new houses are building wherever space can be
found. The population consists of white persons, of mulatto
and black free people, and of slaves also of several shades.

Recife is a thriving place, increasing daily in opulence
and importance. The prosperity which it enjoys may be in
some measure attributed to the character of its Governor
and Captain-General, Caetano Pinto de Miranda Monte-
negro, who has ruled the province for the last ten years
with systematic steadiness and uniform prudence. He has
made no unnecessary innovations, but he has allowed useful improvements to be introduced. He has not interfered
and intermeddled with those concerns in which govern-
ments have no business, but he has supported them when
they have been once established. I here speak of commercial regulations and minor improvements in the chief
town, and in the smaller settlements of the country. He is
affable, and hears the complaint of a peasant or a rich

merchant with the same patience; he is just, seldom exercising the power which he possesses of punishing without appeal to the civil magistrate; and when he does enforce it, the crime must be very glaring indeed. He acts upon a system, and from principle; and if it is the fate of Brazil to be in the hands of a despotic government, happy, compared to its present state, would it in general be, if all its rulers resembled him. I love the place at which I so long resided, and I hope most sincerely that he may not be removed, but that he may continue to dispense to that extensive region the blessings of a mild, forbearing administration.

In political consequence, with reference to the Portuguese government, Pernambuco holds the third rank amongst the provinces of Brazil; but in a commercial point of view, with reference to Great Britain, I know not whether it should not be named first. Its chief exports are cotton and sugar; the former mostly comes to England. The latter is chiefly shipped to Lisbon. Hides, coconuts, ipecacuanha and a few other drugs are exported in trifling quantities. These articles are exchanged for manufactured goods, earthenware, porter, and other articles of necessity among civilized people, and also of luxury to no very great amount. Two or three ships sail annually for Goa in the East Indies; and the trade to the coast of Africa for slaves is considerable. Several vessels from the United States arrive at Recife annually, bringing flour, of which great quantities are now consumed; furniture for dwelling houses, and other kinds of lumber, and carrying away sugar, molasses and rum. During the late war between the United States and England, which interrupted this trade, Recife was at first somewhat distressed for wheat-flour, but a supply arrived from Rio Grande do Sul, the most southern province of the kingdom of Brazil. The quality is good, and I rather think that some coasting-vessels will continue to supply the market with this article, notwithstanding the renewed communication with North America.

II

SOCIETY AND FESTIVALS

The first few days after my arrival were spent in delivering my letters of introduction. I soon became acquainted with all the English merchants, who live in a very respectable style, and have done much good in establishing some customs which the Portuguese have had the sense to follow, preserving at the same time those of their own which are fitted to the country and the climate.

As this was the summer season, great numbers of the inhabitants were out of town; they remove to small cottages at Olinda, and upon the banks of the rivers, to enjoy a purer air, and the amusement and comfort of bathing, during the months most subject to hot, parching weather. The heat is, however, seldom very oppressive: the sea breeze, during the whole year, commences about nine o'clock in the morning, and continues until midnight. At the time this subsides the land breeze rises, and continues until early in the morning, and the half hour in the forenoon which occasionally passes between the one and the other is the most unpleasant period of the day. In the rainy season, just before the commencement of a heavy shower, the clouds are very dark, dense, and low; the breeze is suspended for a short time; there is then a sort of expectant stillness, and the weather is very sultry.

One afternoon I rode out with several young men to a village in the neighborhood, for the purpose of delivering a letter to one of the rich merchants. We passed through Boa Vista, and proceeded along a narrow sandy road, formed by frequent passing and repassing; and along the sides of this are many of the summer residences of the wealthy inhabitants of the town, which are small, neat, whitewashed cottages of one floor, with gardens in front and at the sides, planted with orange, lemon, pomegranate, and many other kinds of fruit trees; some few are enclosed partly by low walls, but for the most part they are protected by fences of timber.

Our English flat saddles created as much surprise to the people of Pernambuco, as those of the Portuguese appeared strange to us. They are high before and behind, which obliges the rider to sit very upright, and the fashion is to be as stiff as possible, and to hold quite perpendicularly a switch of most enormous length. The horses are taught a delightful amble, upon which some of them can be made to proceed with great speed.

A Portuguese friend, with whom I had been acquainted in England, having taken a house at Poço da Panella, I agreed to share the expense of it with him, and we immediately removed to it, to pass the summer months. The village was quite full; not a hut remained untenanted; and, as occurs in England at watering places, families, whose dwellings in town are spacious and handsome, regardless of inconvenience, came to reside here during the summer in very small cottages. Poço da Panella contains a chapel, built by subscription, a row of houses running parallel with the river, several washer-women's huts in front of them, and other dwellings scattered about in all directions. Here the ceremonious manners of the town are thrown aside, and exchanged for an equal degree of freedom. Our mornings were filled up, either in riding to Recife or to some other part of the country, or in conversation at the houses of any of the families with whom we were acquainted; and the afternoons and evenings with music, dancing, playing at forfeits, or in dining with some of the English merchants, a few of whom had also removed to this place and its neighborhood. At many of the Portuguese houses I found the card tables occupied at nine o'clock in the morning; when one person rose another took his place; and thus they were scarcely deserted, except during the heat of the day, when each man either returned to his own home to dine, or, as is much less frequent, was requested to remain and partake with the family.

On the last day of this year I was invited to visit

Olinda, that I might witness the festival of Our Lady of the Mountain. Olinda covers much ground, but contains only about 4,000 inhabitants. At this time the whole city presented a scene of bustle and amusement. The church, particularly decorated on this occasion, stands upon the highest point; the assemblage of persons was great; the church was lighted up, and a few individuals of both sexes were kneeling promiscuously in the body of it, but the service was over.

This is the season of cheerfulness and gaiety, and we were likewise to have our festival at Poço da Panella. These festivals are always preceded by nine evenings of hymn-singing, and music, in honor of the Virgin, or the saint whose day is to be thus celebrated. On this occasion the performance for the *novena*, or nine evenings, consisted of a piano-forte played by a lady, the wife of a merchant, and a guitar, and some wind instruments, played by several young men of respectability. The vocal music was also executed by the same persons, assisted by some female mulatto slaves belonging to the lady. I was somewhat surprised to hear the airs of country-dances and marches occasionally introduced. However, on the day of the festival, the performers were professional men, and in the evening fireworks were displayed. Every house in the village was crowded this day with people from all parts. My friend and I had several persons to dinner, but before we had half finished, some of *their* friends appeared, and without ceremony came in and helped themselves; soon all idea of regularity vanished, and things were scrambled for. In a short time both of us left our own house, and tried to gain admittance to some other, but all were in the same confusion. We were invited to a dance in the evening, at which the Governor was present; and although he is himself desirous of making every person feel at ease, still such is the dreadful idea of rank, for I know not what else to call it, in this country, that the behavior of every one was constrained, and the conversation carried on almost in a whisper.

I lost no festivals, and amongst others, went to that

of Santo Amaro, the healer of wounds, at whose chapel
are sold bits of ribbon, as charms, which many individuals
of the lower orders of people tie round their naked ankles
or their wrists, and preserve until they wear out, and drop
off.

About the commencement of Lent, the villages in the
neighborhood are almost entirely deserted by the white
people, who return to town to see the processions customary at this season in Catholic countries. The rains also
usually begin about the end of March. I did not leave Poço
da Panella until the very last, but in the end found the
place dull, and followed the rest.

On Holy Thursday, accompanied by two of my
countrymen, I sallied forth at three o'clock, to see the
churches, which are, on this occasion, lighted up, and
highly ornamented. The whole town was in motion; the
females, too, both high and low, were this afternoon
parading the streets on foot, contrary to their usual custom; many of them were dressed in silks of different colors,
and covered with gold chains and other trinkets, a general
muster being made of all the finery that could be collected.
The blaze in some of the churches, from great numbers of
wax tapers, was prodigious; the object apparently aimed
at was the production of the greatest quantity of light, as
in some instances mirrors were fixed behind the tapers.
The middle of the body of these churches is completely
open; there are no pews, no distinction of places; the principal chapel is invariably at the opposite end from the
chief entrance, recedes from the church, and is narrower;
this part is appropriated to the officiating priests, and is
railed in from the body of the church. The females, as they
enter, whether white or of color, place themselves as near
to the rails as they can, squatting down upon the floor of
the large open space in the center. The men stand along
either side of the body of the church, a narrow slip, being
in most instances railed off lengthways; or they remain
near to the entrance, behind the women; but every female,
of whatever rank or color, is first accommodated.

On the following day, Good Friday, the decorations
of the churches, the dress of the women, and even the
manner of both sexes, was changed; all was dismal. In the
morning I went with the same gentlemen to the church of
the Sacramento, to witness a representation of our Saviour's descent from the Cross. We entered the church by a
side door; it was much crowded, and the difficulty of
getting in was considerable. An enormous curtain hung
from the ceiling, excluding from the sight the whole of the
principal chapel. An Italian missionary friar of the Penha
convent, with a long beard, and dressed in a thick dark
brown cloth habit, was in the pulpit, and about to commence an extempore sermon. After an exordium of some
length, adapted to the day, he cried out "Behold him";
the curtain immediately dropped, and discovered an
enormous Cross, with a full-sized wooden image of our
Saviour, exceedingly well carved and painted, and around
it a number of angels represented by several young persons, all finely decked out, and each bearing a large pair
of out-stretched wings, made of gauze; a man, dressed in
a bog wig, and pea-green robe, as St. John, and a female
kneeling at the foot of the Cross, as the Magdalen; whose
character, as I was informed, seemingly that nothing
might be wanting, was not the most pure. The friar continued, with much vehemence, and much action, his narrative of the crucifixion, and after some minutes, again
cried out, "Behold, they take him down"; when four
men, habited in imitation of Roman soldiers, stepped for-
wards. The countenances of these persons were in part
concealed by black crape. Two of them ascended ladders
placed on each side against the Cross, and one took down
the board, bearing the letters I. N. R. I. Then was removed the crown of thorns, and a white cloth was put
over, and pressed down upon the head; which was soon
taken off, and shown to the people, stained with the circular mark of the crown in blood: this done, the nails which
transfix the hands were by degrees knocked out, and this
produced a violent beating of breasts among the female

part of the congregation. A long white linen bandage was next passed under each armpit of the image; the nail which secured the feet was removed; the figure was let down very gently, and was carefully wrapped up in a white sheet. All this was done by word of command from the preacher. The sermon was then quickly brought to a conclusion, and we left the church.

On Saturday morning we were saluted with the bellowing of cattle, the grunting of pigs, and the cries of the Negro slaves with baskets of fowls of several kinds for sale; these were to be devoured after the ensuing midnight, and many families, weary of their long abstinence, impatiently awaited the striking of the clocks, as a signal for the commencement of hostile operations, without mercy or scruple, upon turkeys, pigs, etc. and all the rest of the lawful victims of our carnivorous nature.

On Easter Sunday I was invited by a physician to dine with him, and to attend the christening of one of his grandchildren. At dinner the party was small; the dishes were served up two at a time to the number of ten or twelve, of all of which I was obliged to taste. From the table we adjourned to the church about four o'clock, where several persons, likewise invited, waited for us; the ceremony was performed by a friar, and each guest held a wax taper, forming a semicircle towards the altar; from hence we returned to the old gentleman's house to supper. I met here, among others belonging to the same convent, the friar who preached the crucifixion sermon. The members of this convent are all Italians and missionaries, but as no reinforcement has for a length of time come out from Europe, very few now remain. A long table was laid out, loaded with victuals. Several ladies were present, notwithstanding which enormous quantities of wine were drunk, until the whole company began to be riotous but still the ladies did not move. At last no order was left among them, bottles and glasses were overturned and broken in the vehement wishes expressed for the prosperity of the whole family of our host, both old and young; when in the midst of this, I escaped about nine o'clock, accompanied by a Franciscan friar. We had a journey in contemplation for the next day, and thought it high time to get away. Parties of this kind are not frequent, and in a general way these people live in a very quiet manner. The old doctor is a native of Lisbon, and a great friend to Englishmen; he was young at the time of the great earthquake, and says he shall never forget that he was in part clothed from the necessaries sent out by the British government for the assistance of the Portuguese after that dreadful calamity.

On the following afternoon, the friar, myself, and a servant, proceeded to Igaraçu, a small town distant from Recife seven leagues, for the purpose of witnessing the entrance of a novice into the Order of St. Francis. We arrived about nine o'clock at night at the gates of the convent; the friar rang the bell three times, as the signal of the arrival of one of the order; a lay brother came, and asked who it was that demanded admittance; he was answered, that it was brother Joseph from the convent of Recife accompanied by a friend; the porter shut the gates again, but soon returned, saying that the Guardian, the name given to the principal of a Franciscan convent, allowed us to enter. We were conducted up a flight of steps into a long corridor, at the end of which sat the Guardian, to whom we were introduced; he directed us to the brother who had the management of the accommodations for visitors; this man placed us under the especial care of Frei Luiz, who took us to his cell. The convents of St. Francis are all built exactly upon the same plan; in the form of a quadrangle, one side of which is appropriated to the church, and the remaining three to cells and to other purposes; the former are above, and to be entered from a gallery, which runs round the whole building. The beds with which the friars supplied us were hard, but very acceptable after our ride.

The ceremony to be performed on the ensuing morning collected great numbers of persons from all quarters, as it is now very rare. Formerly, of every family at least one member was a friar, but now this is not the custom; children are brought up to trade, to the army, to any thing rather than to a monastic life, which is fast losing its reputation. None of the convents are full, and some of them are nearly without inhabitants.

Early in the morning the church was lighted up, and about ten o'clock the family of the person about to take the vows arrived to occupy the seats prepared for them. Mass was then said, and a sermon preached; about eleven o'clock the novice, a young man of sixteen years of age, entered the principal chapel by a side door, walking between two brothers, with a large cross in his hands, and dressed in a long dark blue robe: there was then much chanting, after which he knelt down opposite to the Guardian, received the usual admonitions, was asked several questions relating to his belief in the doctrines of the church, and then made the separate vows, of defending his religion, of celibacy, and others of minor importance. The Guardian then dressed him in the habit of the order, made of very thick, rough, dark brown cloth, which before lay stretched upon the ground in front of the altar, covered with flowers; this being done, the young man embraced all the brothers present, took leave of his relations, and left the church. Many of the friars were laughing during the ceremony, and were particularly amused at the Guardian accidentally saying, "Brother, don't be ashamed"; owing to the young man being much abashed. A visitor who stood near to me in the gallery, from which there are windows into the church, said, in a low voice to be heard only by those immediately around him; "See your chief himself thus advises him to put shame aside, which unfortunately you are all too much inclined to do"; at this the friars who were within hearing all laughed. Great part of the community and many other persons dined with the father of the young friar, and I among the rest; there was much eating, much drinking, and much confusion. In the evening fireworks were displayed, which ended by a transparency, representing a novice receiving the benediction of his Guardian.

We were invited to pass the following Sunday with this family, which consisted of the father and mother, and a son and daughter; they were all Brazilians, and though the young lady had never been from Pernambuco, her manners were easy, and her conversation lively and entertaining. Her complexion was not darker than that of the Portuguese in general, her eyes and hair black, and her features on the whole good; her figure small, but well shaped. Though I have seen others handsomer, still this lady may be accounted a very fair sample of the white Brazilian females; but it is among the women of color that the finest persons are to be found—more life and spirit, more activity of mind and body; they are better fitted to the climate, and the mixed race seems to be its proper inhabitant. Their features, too, are often good, and even the color, which in European climates is disagreeable, appears to appertain to that in which it more naturally exists; but this bar to European ideas of beauty set aside, finer specimens of the human form cannot be found than among the mulatto females whom I have seen.

We went to them to breakfast, which was of coffee and cakes. Backgammon and cards were then introduced until dinner time, at two o'clock. This consisted of great numbers of dishes, placed upon the table without any arrangement, and brought in without any regard to the regularity of courses. We were, as may be supposed, rather surprised at being complimented with pieces of meat from the plates of various persons at the table. I have often met with this custom, particularly amongst families in the interior, and this I now speak of had only resided in Recife a short time; but many of the people of the town have other ideas on these matters. Two or three knives only were placed upon the table, which obliged each person to cut all the meat upon his own plate into small pieces, and pass the knife to his next neighbor. There was, however, a plentiful supply of silver forks, and abundance of plates. Garlic formed one ingredient in almost every dish, and we had a great deal of wine during the dinner. The conversation was trifling, but entertaining; there was much wit and sport. The ladies of the house, joined by several others in the evening, talked a great deal, and would allow of no subject into which they could not enter.

It will be observed from what I have described, and from what I still have to mention, that no rule can be laid down for the society of the place in question; families of equal rank, and of equal wealth and importance, are often of manners totally different. The fact is, that society is undergoing a rapid change.

On St. Anne's day, the 29th July, two young Englishmen and myself proceeded by invitation to the house of one of the first personages of Pernambuco; a man possessing three sugar works in different parts of the country. This was the anniversary of the birthday of our hostess; but the females were all ushered into one room, and the men into another; cards and backgammon, as usual, were the amusements, but there was little of ease and freedom of conversation. At dinner, the ladies all arranged themselves on one side, and the men opposite to them; there were victuals of many kinds in great profusion, and much wine was drunk. Some of the gentlemen who were intimately acquainted with the family did not sit down at table, but assisted in attending upon the ladies. After dinner, the whole party adjourned into a large hall, and country dancing being proposed and agreed to, fiddlers were introduced, and a little after seven o'clock, about twenty couples commenced, and continued this amusement until past two o'clock.

The rains this season had been very slight, and I was tempted by the fineness of the weather to remove entirely to a small cottage in the vicinity, where my time passed away pleasantly, though quietly, and in a manner very barren of events.

I had an offer of introduction to another Brazilian family, which I readily accepted, and on the 7th August I was summoned by my friend to accompany him to Olinda. The family consisted of an old lady, her two daughters, and a son, who is a priest, and one of the professors or masters of the seminary. Several persons of the same class were present, of easy and gentlemanlike manners; some of them proposed dancing, and although they did not join in the amusement, still they were highly pleased to see others entertained in this manner. Our music was a piano-forte, played by one of the professors, who good-humoredly continued until the dancers themselves begged him to desist.

Three or four families are in the practice of having weekly evening card parties, as was usual in Lisbon. I attended these occasionally, but in them there was no peculiarity of customs.

It was the custom in Pernambuco to uncover when passing a sentinel, or on meeting a guard of soldiers marching through the streets. Soon after the opening of the port to British shipping, three English gentlemen accidentally met a corporal's guard of four or five men, and as they passed each other, one of the latter took off the hat of one of the former, accompanying the action by an opprobrious expression; the Englishmen resented the insult, attacked and absolutely routed the guard. This dreadful mark of submission to military power was universally refused by every British subject, and has been very much discontinued even by the Portuguese. Another annoyance to these visitors was the usual respect paid to the Sacrament, carried with much pomp and ceremony to persons dangerously ill. It was expected that everyone by whom it chanced to pass should kneel, and continue in that posture until it was out of sight; here Englishmen, in some degree, conformed in proper deference to the religion of the country, but the necessity of this also is wearing off.

III

Governmental
Institutions

The captaincies-general, or provinces of the first rank, in Brazil, of which Pernambuco is one, are governed by captains-general or governors, who are appointed for three years. At the end of this period the same person is continued or not, at the option of the supreme government. They are, in fact, absolute in power.

The ecclesiastical government is scarcely connected with that above-mentioned, and is administered by a bishop and a dean and chapter, with his vicar-general, etc. The governor cannot even appoint a chaplain to the island of Fernando de Noronha, one of the dependencies of Pernambuco, but acquaints the bishop that a priest is wanted, who then nominates one for the place.

The number of civil and military officers is enormous; inspectors innumerable, colonels without end, devoid of any objects to inspect, without any regiments to command; judges to manage each trifling department, of which the duties might all be done by two or three persons; thus salaries are augmented; the people are oppressed, but the state is not benefited.

Taxes are laid where they fall heavy upon the lower classes, and none are levied where they could well be borne. A tenth is raised in kind upon cattle, poultry, and agriculture, and even upon salt; this in former times appertained, as in other Christian countries, to the clergy. All the taxes are farmed to the highest bidders, and this among the rest. They are parcelled out in extensive districts, and are contracted for at a reasonable rate, but the contractors again dispose of their shares in small portions; these are again retailed to other persons, and as a profit is obtained by each transfer the people must be oppressed, that these men may satisfy those above them and enrich

themselves. Every transfer of immovable property is subject to a duty of ten per cent and movables to five per cent.
Besides these, there are many other taxes of minor importance. Rum, both for exportation and home consumption, pays a duty of 80 *reis per canada*, which is sometimes
a fourth of its value, but may be reckoned as from fifteen
to twenty per cent. Cotton pays the tenth, and is again
taxed at the moment of exportation 600 *reis per arroba* of
32 lbs. or about 1 1/4*d.* per lb. Nothing can be more in-
judicious than this double duty upon the chief article of
exportation. The duties at the customhouse are fifteen
per cent upon imports, of which the valuation is left in
some measure to the merchant to whom the property
belongs.

Now, although the expenses of the provincial govern-
ments are great, and absorb a very considerable proportion of the receipts, owing to the number of officers employed in every department, still the salaries of each are,
in most instances, much too small to afford a comfortable
subsistence; consequently peculation, bribery, and other
crimes of the same description are to be looked for, and
they become so frequent as to escape all punishment or
even notice; though there are some men whose character
is without reproach.

The public institutions are not many, but, of those
that exist, some are excellent. The seminary at Olinda for
the education of young persons is well conducted, and
many of its professors are persons of knowledge and of
liberality. Free schools are also established in most of the
small towns in the country, in some of which the Latin
language is taught, but the major part are adapted only to
give instruction in reading, writing and arithmetic. Neither in these nor in the seminary is any expense incurred
by the pupils. The Lazarus Hospital is neglected, but
patients are admitted; the other establishments for the
sick are very miserable.

The friars are not numerous, though they are far too
much so. These useless beings amount to about one

hundred and fifty in number at Olinda, Recife, Igaraçu, and Paraíba. But there are no nuns in the province, though of the establishments called *Recolhimentos* or Retreats, three exist. These are directed by elderly females, who have not taken any vows, and who educate young persons of their own sex, and receive individuals whose conduct has been incorrect, but whose characters are not notorious, and who are placed here by their relations to prevent further shame. The number of churches, chapels, and niches in the streets for saints, is quite preposterous; to these are attached a multitude of religious lay brotherhoods, of which the members are merchants, and other persons in trade, and even some are composed of mulatto and black free people. Some of these continually beg for a supply of wax, and other articles to be consumed in honor of their patron. Almost every day in the year, passengers are importuned in the streets, and the inhabitants in their houses, by some of these people, and among others, by the lazy Franciscan friars.

It will appear surprising to English persons that in a place so large as Recife there should be no printing press or bookseller. At the convent of the *Madre de Deus*, are sold almanacs, prints and histories of the Virgin and saints, and other productions of the same description, but of very limited size, printed at Lisbon. The post office is conducted in a very irregular manner. There is no established means of forwarding letters to any part of the interior of the country, nor along the coast, so that the post office merely receives the letter bags which are brought by the small vessels that trade with other ports along this coast, and sends the bags from Pernambuco by the same conveyances; and as there is not any regular delivery of letters, each person must inquire for his own at the office. There is a theater of Recife, in which are performed Portuguese farces, but the establishment is most wretchedly conducted.

The Botanic Garden at Olinda is one of those institutions which have arisen from the removal of the Court to South America. I much fear, however, that the zeal shown at the commencement has somewhat cooled. A botanist has been appointed with an adequate salary. He is a Frenchman, who had resided at Cayenne, and with this choice many persons were much dissatisfied, as it was thought, and with good reason, that a Portuguese subject might have been found quite capable of taking the management of the garden.

The sight, of all others, the most offensive to an Englishman, is that of the criminals, who perform the menial offices of the palace, the barracks, the prisons, and other public buildings. They are chained in couples, and each couple is followed by a soldier, armed with a bayonet. The prisons are in a very bad state, little attention being paid to the situation of their inhabitants. Executions are rare at Pernambuco; the more usual punishment inflicted, even for crimes of the first magnitude, is transportation to the coast of Africa. White persons must be removed for trial to Baía, for crimes of which the punishment is death. Even to pass sentence of death upon a man of color, or a Negro, several judicial officers must be present. There does not exist here a regular police; when an arrest is to be effected in Recife or its neighborhood, two officers of justice are accompanied by soldiers, from one or other of the regiments of the line, for this purpose. A *ronda* or patrol, consisting of soldiers, parades the streets during the night, at stated periods, but it is not of much service to the town.

The military establishment is much neglected. The regular troops consist of two regiments of infantry, which ought to form together a body of 2,500 men, but they seldom collect more effectives than 600; so that sufficient numbers can scarcely be mustered to do the duty of the town of Recife, of Olinda, and the forts. Their pay is less than 2 3/4*d.* per day, and a portion of the flour of the manioc weekly, and their clothing is afforded to them very irregularly. From their miserable pay, rather more than one farthing per day is held back for a religious purpose. Recruits are made of some of the worst individuals in the

province; this mode of recruiting, and their most wretched
pay, account completely for the depreciated character of
the soldiers of the line. They are formed chiefly of Brazilians, and people of color. Besides these regiments, the
militia of the town sometimes do duty without pay, and
these make but a sorry show. The militia regiments, commanded by mulatto and black officers, and formed entirely of men of these castes, are very superior in appearance.

There is one political arrangement of this province
which, above all others, cries aloud for alteration. I speak
of the small island of Fernando de Noronha. To this spot
are transported, for a number of years or for life, a great
number of male criminals. No females are permitted to
visit the island. The garrison, consisting of about 120 men,
is relieved yearly. It is a very difficult matter to obtain a
priest to serve for a twelvemonth, as chaplain in the island.

The supineness of the ancient system upon which
Brazil was ruled is still too apparent throughout; but the
removal of the Sovereign to that country has roused many
persons who had been long influenced by habits of in-
dolence, and has increased the activity of others who have
impatiently awaited a field for its display. The Brazilians
feel of more importance, their native soil now gives law to
the mother-country; their spirit, long kept under severe
subjection to ancient colonial rules and regulations, has
now had some opportunities of showing itself—has proved,
that though of long suffering, and patient of endurance, it
does exist, and that if its possessors are not treated as men
instead of children, it will break forth, and rend asunder
those shackles to which they have forbearingly submitted.
I hope, however, most sincerely, that the supreme government may see the necessity of reformation, and that the
people will not expect too much, but consider that many
hardships are preferable to a generation of bloodshed,
confusion, and misery.

Freedom of communication with other nations has
already been of service to the country, and the benefits
which it imparts are daily augmenting. This shoot from

our European continent will ultimately increase, and a plant will spring up, infinitely more important than the branch from which it proceeded; and though the season of its maturity is far distant, yet the rapidity of its advance or tardiness of its growth greatly depends upon the fostering care or indifferent negligence of its rulers. Still, whatever the conduct of these may be, its extent, its fertility, and other numerous advantages must, in the course of time, give to it that rank which it has a right to claim among the great nations of the world.

IV

To Paraíba and Natal

I had much desired to perform some considerable journey into the less populous and less cultivated part of the country, and discovered that the brother of a gentleman resident at Goiana, was about to set off for that place, and would, probably, from thence proceed further into the country, with some object in view connected with trade. It was my intention to advance as far as Ceará. I applied to the governor for a passport, which was immediately granted without any difficulty.

On the 19th October, 1810, my companion arrived, bringing with him his black guide. Preparations were made for proceeding upon our journey, and about one o'clock, as the moon rose, we sallied forth, Senhor Feliz, myself, and my English servant John on horseback, armed with swords and pistols; the black guide also on horseback, without saddle or bridle, carrying a blunderbuss, and driving on before him a baggage-horse, with a little mulatto boy mounted between the panniers. That part of the road which we traversed by moonlight I had already passed over a short time before, and subsequently, from frequent travelling, my acquaintance with it was such that I might have become a guide upon it.

We rode along a sandy path for three quarters of a league, until we began to ascend a steep hill, of which the sides and the flat summit are covered with large trees, and thick brushwood growing beneath them. The hamlet of Beberibe stands at the foot of the corresponding declivity; to this place several families resort in the summer, and a small rivulet runs through it, of which the water is most beautifully clear. Half a league beyond Beberibe we crossed another rivulet, and immediately afterward commenced our ascent of the hill of Quebraçu, which is in most parts very steep and very narrow, being enclosed on one side by a precipice, and on the other by sloping ground covered with wood. This ridge of hill is quite flat along the top, and the path continues for half a league, between lofty trees and impenetrable brushwood. We descended into the long and narrow valley of Merueira, through which a rivulet runs, of which the water never fails. The ascent, on the opposite side of this beautiful vale, is very steep; the path along the summit of the ridge is similar to that over which we had travelled; we soon again descended, and on our arrival at the bottom, entered the long, straggling village of Paratibe, with manioc lands and plantain and tobacco gardens intermixed with the houses. The inhabitants are mostly laboring free persons, white, mulatto, and black. The houses are built on each side of the road at intervals, for the distance of one mile. A rivulet runs through it, which in the rainy season often overflows its banks to a considerable distance on each side. Beyond this village the road is comparatively flat, but is still diversified by unequal small elevations; several sugarworks are seen, and great numbers of small cottages; the passing of the country people with loaded horses, carrying cotton, hides, and other articles, the produce of the country, and returning with many kinds of wares, salt meat, and fish from Recife, may almost be called continual.

The town of Igaraçu, which we now entered, is one of the oldest settlements upon this part of the coast, and stands at the distance of two leagues from the sea upon the banks of a creek. The place plainly denotes that it has enjoyed greater prosperity than it at present has to boast of; many of the houses are of two stories, but they are neglected, and some of the small cottages are in decay and ruin. The streets are paved, but are much out of repair, and grass grows in many of them. It contains several churches, one convent, and a *recolhimento* or retreat for females, a town hall, and prison. The only regular inn of which the country has to boast is established here, for the convenience of passengers between Recife and Goiana,

and at this we intended to have stopped, had not the early
hour at which we reached it, tempted us to push forward
before the sun became more powerful.

The road continues flat and sandy, and two leagues
beyond Igaraçu we entered the village of Pasmado, which
is built in the form of a square; it consists of a church and
a number of cottages. We proceeded through it, crossed
the most considerable stream we had yet seen this day,
called Araripe. We ascended another steep hill, passed
several sugarworks and cottages, and crossed several rivu-
lets, traversing a most delightful country. We rode through
the hamlets of Bû and Fontainhas, at the former of which
there is a chapel. From the latter the road is chiefly over a
sandy plain, almost without wood, until the *engenho* of
Bujiri is discovered with its field of grass and woods around.
Immediately beyond we forded the river of Goiana, and
in a few minutes more entered the town of Goiana, between four and five o'clock in the afternoon. The distance
from Recife to Goiana is fifteen leagues.

The road we had travelled over is the highway from
the sertão, by which the cattle descend from the estates
upon the river Açu, and from the plains of this portion of
the interior to the markets of Recife; therefore the continued passing of large droves of cattle has beat down the
underwood, and made a broad sandy road; the large trees
still remain, if it has so happened that any grew upon the
track; these, if of any size, brave the crowd of animals, and
will remain either until they decay from age and fall, or till
regular roads begin to be constructed in Brazil. Thus, if
the ground is flat, the road is not bad; but upon the sides
of hills, instead of being carried round the steepest ascents,
the track has been made straight up and down or nearly
so, and the winter torrents form deep caverns and ravines,
the sides of which sometimes fall in and make the roads
very dangerous; so that, unless well acquainted with a hill,
it is by no means safe to ascend or descend by night, as one
or two days of the usual rain of Brazil may have made a
great difference, and have rendered the road impassable.

I was received most kindly by Senhor Joaquim, whom I had before had the pleasure of meeting at Recife, and he was not a man to be long in becoming acquainted with. We sat down to dinner about five o'clock, when his lady and two little girls, his daughters, made their appearance. We had dishes cooked in Portuguese, Brazilian, and English style.

Senhor Joaquim had business at Paraíba, which he intended to have sent his brother Felix to transact; but as I offered to accompany him, he thought it would be pleasant to go with me, and show the lions of that city. We sent off his black guide and my servant with a loaded horse before us, and followed the next day with his black boy. The road between Goiana and Paraíba presents nothing particularly interesting—the hills are steep but not high, and woods, plantations, and cottages are, as usual, the objects to be seen. The distance is thirteen leagues. We entered the city of Paraíba at twelve o'clock.

The city of Paraíba (for much smaller places even than this bear the rank of city in these yet thinly peopled regions) contains from two to three thousand inhabitants, including the lower town. It bears strong marks of having been a place of more importance than it is now, and though some improvements were going on, they were conducted entirely through the means which government supplied for them, or rather, the governor wished to leave some memorial of his administration of the province. The principal street is broad and paved with large stones, but is somewhat out of repair. The houses are mostly of one story, with the ground floors as shops, and a few of them have glass windows; an improvement which has been only lately introduced into Recife. The Jesuits' convent is employed as the governor's palace, and the *ouvidor*'s office and residence also; the church of the convent stands in the center, and these are the two wings. The convents of the Franciscan, Carmelite, and Benedictine Orders are very large buildings, and are almost uninhabited; the first contains four or five friars, the second two, and the third only

one. Besides these, the city has to boast of six churches. The
public fountains at Paraíba are the only works of the kind
I met with any where on the part of the coast which I
visited.

The lower town consists of small houses, and is situated upon the borders of a spacious basin or lake, formed
by the junction of three rivers, which from hence discharge
their waters into the sea, by one considerable stream. The
banks of the basin are covered with mangroves, as in all
the salt water rivers of this country.

The trade of Paraíba is inconsiderable, though the
river admits of vessels of 150 tons upon the bar; and when
in the basin, opposite to the lower town, a rope yarn would
keep them still, as no harm could reach them. It contains
a regular customhouse, which is seldom opened.

I soon saw what was to be seen, and we had no society; time, however, did not appear to hang heavy, for
Senhor Joaquim was a man of inexhaustible good humor
and hilarity. We lived by magic, as the colonel had ordered
his servant to supply every thing for us.

I had entertained hopes of being accompanied by
Senhor Joaquim, at least as far as Rio Grande, but he
changed his mind, and I began to make the necessary arrangements for going alone. I purchased three more
horses, and hired a guide for the sertão, who was a white
man of the country, and two Indian lads of about sixteen
years of age. I had with me a trunk with my clothes on one
side of the packsaddle, and a case with some bottles of rum
and wine on the other side, and my hammock in the
middle; these made one load. The other horse carried in
the *malas*, a kind of trunk, on the one side our provisions,
and on the other the clothes of my people, additional ropes,
and other tackle. I was far from being well supplied, but
afterward provided myself with more things as I went on,
learning by experience. The hammocks are all made of
cotton, and are of several sizes and colors, and of various
workmanship. Those in use among the lower orders, are
made of cotton cloth, of the manufacture of the country;

others are composed of network, from which all the several kinds derive the general name of *Rêde*, a net; others, again, are knit or woven in long straight threads, knotted across at intervals; these are usually dyed of two or three colors, and are to be found in the houses of wealthy persons. This species of bed has been adopted from the Indians, and nothing more convenient and better adapted to the climate could possibly be imagined; it can be wrapped up into a very small compass, and, with the addition of a piece of baize as a coverlid, is usually of sufficient warmth.

From Dois Rios we advanced the following day to the sugar plantation of Espirito Santo, situated upon the banks of the river Paraíba, which becomes dry in the summer at a short distance above this estate. I had letters to the owner of it, who is a member of the Cavalcante family, and the capitão-mor of the captaincy of Paraíba. I was received by him in a very friendly manner. The house is in the usual style of the country, having only the ground floor, and no ceiling, the tiles and rafters being in full view. Supper of dried meat, and the flour of the manioc made into paste, and called *pirão*, was placed before me; also some hard biscuits and red wine. I was not then sufficiently a Brazilian to eat *pirão*, and took the biscuits with the meat in preference, which much astonished my host. Sweetmeats were afterward brought in, which are always good in the houses of persons of his rank in life, the opulent people in Brazil taking as much pride in their *doces* as an English citizen in his table or his wines. The cloth was laid at one end of a long table, and I sat down by myself, while the capitão-mor placed himself upon the table, near to the other end, and talked to me; and some of the chief persons of his establishment stood around, to see the strange animal called an Englishman. We adjourned from the supper-room into another spacious apartment, and each of us took a hammock, of which there were several in the room, and swung and talked until we were half asleep.

The capitão-mor seldom leaves his estate to go to Recife, or even to Paraíba, and lives in the usual style of the Brazilian gentry, in a kind of feudal state. He had several young men about him, some of whom were employed by him; neither his wife, nor any of his children appeared. The principal apartments of this house are two spacious rooms, having a great number of doors and windows; in one were several hammocks and a sofa; and in the other, the long table upon which I supped; there were a few chairs in each of them; the floors were of brick, and the shutters and doors were unpainted. The owner of this mansion wore a shirt and a pair of drawers, a long bedgown, called a *chambre*, and a pair of slippers. This is the usual dress of those persons who have no work to perform. When a Brazilian takes to wearing one of these long gowns, he begins to think himself a gentleman, and entitled, consequently, to much respect.

The next day we advanced about seven leagues, and, for the first time, I slept in the open air. We discovered that not far off, a field or piece of land, rather more cleared of wood than the rest, was rented by a cottager, who would allow our horses to be put into it for a *vintém*, about five farthings each, for the night, which the guide thought I should consider dear, and therefore told me it was the usual price. As may be supposed, I made no great difficulties on this score, and the horses were taken to the place by Julio and his companion. I now thought myself settled for the night, and therefore ate my supper, sitting in my hammock, which was slung between two trees, with the plate upon one of the trunks; having finished, I took my cigar, and sat down close to the fire; the guide lighted his pipe, and placed himself on the opposite side, that we might have a talk about our proceedings for the morrow.

This was to me a new scene. I was cheered by my recollection of the knowledge I had of the language, and by the determination I felt within me of conforming to the customs of the people—of submitting to their prejudices. I was not old enough to have contracted any habits too deep to be laid aside when necessary. These thoughts were interrupted by the cry of "Jesus," which was repeated every half minute in a dismal voice; I called to the guide, supposing it to proceed from some person in distress; he waked, and I told him what had made me call to him—he said it was only some person helping another, "*a bem morrer*," that is, that some dying person, which I found was the usual custom, had a friend to repeat the word "Jesus" until the sufferer expired, that it might not be forgotten, and, perhaps, to keep the devil off.

We proceeded to Cunhaû, the sugar plantation of Colonel Andre d'Albuquerque do Maranhão, the chief of the Maranhão branch of this numerous and distinguished family of the Albuquerques. He is a man of immense landed property. The plantation of Cunhaû extends along the road fourteen leagues, and the owner has since purchased another large estate adjoining; his lands likewise in the sertão for breeding cattle are supposed not to be less than thirty to forty leagues in extent—of those kind of leagues that sometimes take a man three or four hours to get over one.

I had letters to him from some of his relations and friends at Pernambuco. He was sitting at his door, with his chaplain and several of his stewards and other persons employed by him, to have all the benefit of the fresh air. He is a man of about thirty years of age, handsome, and rather above the middle size, with genteel manners, rather courtly, as the Brazilians of education generally are. He lives quite in feudal state; his Negroes and other dependents are numerous. He commands the regiment of militia cavalry of Rio Grande, and has them in good order, considering the state of the country. He came forward on my dismounting, and I gave him the letters, which he put by to read at leisure, and then desiring me to sit down, asked me several questions of my wishes, intentions, etc. He took me to his guests' apartments at a little distance from his own residence, where I found a good bed; hot water was brought to me in a large brass basin, and every necessary was supplied in a magnificent style—the towels were all fringed, etc. When I had dressed myself, I expected to be called to supper, but, to my amazement, I waited until near one o'clock, when a servant came to summon me. I found in the dining-room a long table laid out and covered with meat of several kinds, and in quantity sufficient for twenty persons; to this feast the colonel, his chaplain, another person, and myself sat down. When I had tasted until I was quite tired, to my utter dismay another course came on, equally profuse of fowls, pastry, etc., etc. and when this was removed, I had yet a third to go through of at least ten different kinds of sweetmeats. The supper could not have been better cooked or handsomer, if it had been prepared at Recife, and even an English epicure might have found much to please his palate. I was not able to retire to rest until near three o'clock; my bed was most excellent, and I enjoyed it still more from not expecting to find one. In the morning, the colonel would not allow me to leave his house until I had breakfast; tea, coffee, and cakes were brought in, all of which were very good. He then took me to see his horses, and pressed me much to leave my own, and take one of his for my journey, that mine might be in good condition on my return, and he also urged me to leave my pack-horses, and take some of his; but as mine were still all in working order, I declined accepting his offer. These circumstances are mentioned to show the frankness with which strangers are treated. I could not get away before ten o'clock.

As usual, on our arrival by the side of the rivulet, the horses were unloaded, and my hammock was slung for me. I laid down in my clothes, but soon I started up, finding myself uneasy. The guide saw me, and called out, "O sir, you are covered with *carrapatos.*" I then perceived them, and felt still more their bites. Instantly throwing off part of my clothes, but with the remainder upon me I ran into the water, and there began to take them off. The *carrapato* or tick, is a small, flat insect, of a dark brown color; about the size of four pins' heads placed together, it fastens upon the skin, and will in time eat its way into it. It is dangerous to pull it out quickly, when already fixed, for if the head remains, inflammation is not unfrequently the conse-

quence. The point of a heated fork or penknife applied to
the insect, when it is too far advanced into the skin to be
taken out with the hand, will succeed in loosening it.
There is another species of tick of much larger size, and of
a lead color; this is principally troublesome to horses and
horned cattle, that are allowed to run loose in lands which
have been only partially cleared. I have, in some instances,
seen horses that have had such vast numbers upon them as
to have been weakened by the loss of blood which they
have occasioned. The insects of this species of *carrapato*
fasten themselves to the skin, but do not force their way
into it. The hammock had fallen to the ground accidentally when taken from the trunk to be slung, and had thus
picked up these unpleasant visitors.

A young man overtook us, and we entered into conversation. He lived at Papari, a village about half a league
out of the road, and he pressed me so much to accompany
him to sleep at his place, that I agreed. Papari is a deep
and narrow valley, a most delightful situation.

We dined in Brazilian style, upon a table raised about
six inches from the ground, around which we sat or rather
laid down upon mats; we had no forks, and the knives, of
which there were two or three, were intended merely to
sever the larger pieces of meat—the fingers were to do the
rest. I remained at Papari during one entire day, that my
horses might have some respite, that I might purchase
another from Senhor Dionisio, and on poor Julio's
account, whose feet had begun to crack from the dryness
of the sands.

The track of country between Goiana and Espirito
Santo, and indeed even to Cunhaû, keeping at no great
distance from the coast, is appropriated for the most part
to sugar plantations; but many of the Senhores de *Engenho*,
sugar planters, also employ part of their time in raising
cotton. The general feature is of an uncultivated country,
though a great quantity of land is yearly employed. The
system of agriculture is so slovenly, or rather, as there is no
necessity for husbandry of land, from the immensity of the
country, and the smallness of its population, lands are

employed one year, and the next the brushwood is allowed
to grow up, giving thus to every piece of ground that is not
absolutely in use that year, the look of one totally un-
touched, until a person is acquainted, in some measure,
from practice, with the appearance of the several kinds of
land. He will then perceive the difference between brushwood that will not grow because the land is of a barren
kind, and that which is left to rise, that the land may rest
for another crop. From this manner of cultivating their
lands, a plantation requires three or four times more
ground than would otherwise be necessary. The *cercados*,
or fenced pieces of ground, attached to each sugar plantation, upon which are fed the cattle kept for the work of it
are the only spots which bear the look of fields; and even
in these, the brushwood is not always sufficiently cleared
away, unless the proprietor is wealthy and has an abundance of persons upon his estate; otherwise such is the fertility of the soil, that without great care the *cercado* will in
time become a wood. There are several hamlets upon the
road, consisting of three and four cottages, and these are
built of slight timber and leaves of the cabbage-trees;
others have mudwalls, and are covered with these leaves;
and now and then, a house built of mud, with a tiled roof,
is to be seen—this bespeaks a man above the common run
of people.

I arrived about eleven o'clock in the morning at the
city of Natal, situated upon the banks of the Rio Grande,
or Potengi. A foreigner, who might chance to land first at
this place, on his arrival upon the coast of Brazil, would
form a very poor opinion of the state of the population of
the country; for, if places like this are called cities, what
must the towns and villages be; but such a judgment
would not prove correct, for many villages, even of Brazil,
surpass this city; the rank must have been given to it, not
from what it was or is, but from the expectation of what it
might be at some future period. The place may contain
from six to seven hundred persons.

I rode immediately to the palace, as I had letters of

introduction to the Governor, from several of his friends at Pernambuco. He received me in the most cordial manner. The Governor, Francisco de Paula Cavalcante de Albuquerque, is a native of Pernambuco, and a younger brother of the chief of the Cavalcante branch of the Albuquerques.

We visited the church in the evening; all the ladies were handsomely dressed in silks of various colors, and black veils thrown over the head and face. A twelvemonth previous to this period these same persons would have gone to church in petticoats of Lisbon printed cottons, and square pieces of thick cloth over their heads, without stockings, and their shoes down at the heels.

The drought of this year had caused a scarcity of the flour of the manioc—the bread of Brazil, and the price was so high at Recife, Goiana, etc. that those persons of Rio Grande who possessed it began to ship it off for other places; this the governor prohibited; he ordered it to be sold in the market place, at a price equal to the gain the owners would have had by sending it away, and if all was not bought, he took it himself, again giving it out when necessary at the same price.

V

Drought and Indians:
Natal to Ceará

The governor did all in his power to dissuade me from
proceeding further, the drought being so great as to render it not quite prudent; but as I had come so far, I was
resolved, at any rate, to make the attempt. If I had been
certain of being able to undertake the journey at a future
period, it would have been better to have returned, and
to have waited until a more favorable season; but I am rejoiced that I went at that time, as, otherwise, I should
most probably have been under the necessity of foregoing
my plan altogether. Some of the disagreeable circumstances which I met with certainly proceeded from the
rigor of the season.

At Natal, I purchased another horse. I crossed the
river in a canoe, and the horses and men upon *jangadas*; we
were landed upon the new raised road, and immediately
beyond it overtook some persons who were going to the
Lagoa Seca, or dry lake, where I was to purchase maize and
farinha, for crossing the tract of country through which
runs the river Ceará-Mirim. We arrived at the dry lake
about six o'clock in the evening, and put up at one of the
cottages. In the course of the following morning, I made
known my principal errand, and that I likewise wished to
purchase another horse.

We remained at this place during one entire day,
and the next morning set off, intending to sleep at a hamlet, called Pai Paulo. We rested at midday near to a well,
and in the afternoon proceeded. Wells are generally
formed in these parts by digging a hole in the ground, to
the depth of two or three feet, until the water appears; if
a person in the neighborhood of one of them, who takes
water from it, should be nice about these matters, a fence
is made round it, but if not, as is oftener the case, the well

remains open, and the cattle come down to drink at it. These pits or wells are called *cacimbas*. The grass was much burnt up, but still there was plenty of it. In the afternoon we passed over some stony ground—it was the first I had met with, and it was very painful to the horses which had come from the sandy soil of Pernambuco; but we soon entered upon a long, though narrow plain, bounded by brushwood, over which the road was clear, and the grass burnt up entirely on each side.

We halted at the place appointed, upon an immense plain; the grass was all gone, and even the hardy trees, the acaju and mangaba, seemed to feel the want of water, for their leaves had begun to fall. The poor horses were taken to a dell at some distance, to try to pick up what they could find, that had escaped the drought and the traveller. Our allowance of water was not large, and therefore we were afraid of eating much salt meat; we did not pass the night comfortably, for the wind rose, and scattered our fires, nor did we sleep much, and at four o'clock the horses were fetched to give to each of them a feed of maize. One of them refused to eat his portion.

The following morning we advanced to Pai Paulo, three leagues further, still crossing the same plain, at the extremity of which we first approached the Ceará-Mirim, and on the opposite side from that on which we were, stands the village of Pai Paulo, upon rising ground. We passed Pai Paulo, and about noon reached an open well of brackish water, dug in the bed of the river; our Pernambuco horses at first refused to drink, but the dirt was cleared away, as much as possible, for them, and the water left to settle; however, even then, they did little more than taste it. Here we were to rest, and to give our horses some maize, for there was no grass.

The following day we proceeded again in the same manner. We reached another dirty pool or well of water in the river, which we had again crossed several times. Our resting place at midday afforded no shelter, excepting what could be obtained from one small shrub, which

was in full leaf. The leaves or branches of it reached to the
ground. I lay down upon the sand, and pushed my head
in among them, covering the rest of my body with a hide;
this was a hot berth, but better than to be completely exposed to the sun. I was astonished at the appearance of
this shrub. There are two kinds of trees in certain parts of
the sertão, which are called Pereiro and Yco; both seem
to flourish most when the seasons are the driest, and both
are particularly dangerous to horses; that is, as they do no
mischief to the wild cattle or wild horses, they may be supposed not to possess any pernicious qualities if the animals
which eat their leaves are not overheated and fatigued;
the latter of these plants kills the travellers' beasts, and the
former has the effect of appearing to produce intoxication, and sometimes also proves fatal. The major said that
this part of the country abounded in these trees, and consequently our horses were tied to those around us, and to
each was given a feed of maize. The plant, of which I have
spoken above, was very beautiful, the green of its leaves
was bright and healthy, and I afterwards saw many more
of them upon this *travessia* or crossing. I particularly observed them on this tract of country, as other plants had
lost all appearance of life.

We were less unpleasantly situated at night, as the
water, though brackish, was comparatively clear.

The following day we had still the same country and
river to cross. The consciousness of having advanced upon
our journey alone caused the knowledge of a change of
situation, so exactly similar was the face of the country.
At midday we had again no shelter from the sun. The
water was little different from that of the preceding day.
We carried water from the resting place at midday, and,
as usual, fixed our quarters at night upon the banks of the
river.

The next day we advanced again exactly in the same
manner, but at noon, to our dismay, there was no water;
the pool had dried up, but we rested the horses for a short
time, notwithstanding this dreadful disappointment. My

thirst was great, for I had not drunk the night before. We had still some lemons left, which were distributed, and these afforded much relief. This was a dismal day, and we knew not whether we should be able to reach a well before some of our horses failed.

The next morning, about nine o'clock, we reached a well to our great joy, but, fortunately for us, the water was so bad that we could not drink much; it was as usual dirty and brackish, but of the first draught I shall never forget the delight—when I tried a second, I could not take it, the taste was so very nauseous. On looking around, we saw some goats. Julio went toward them, and then discovered some fowls, proceeded a little farther and found an inhabited cottage. He came and gave us the joyful intelligence; we determined to remain here to rest, if the people could give us any hopes of food for our horses. I found an elderly woman and her two daughters in the hut; the father was not at home. The old woman seemed quite astonished to hear that we had crossed the Ceará-Mirim; she said, she did not know how soon she and her family might be obliged to leave their cottage, as many others had done. She directed the major and my people to a dell at some distance, where dry grass and leaves might perhaps still be picked up; she said that it was the last place which could have any, for travellers did not in general know of it, and she and her husband made a point of not discovering it. But I paved the way, by making her a present of some *farinha*, throwing maize to the fowls, and by pouring in an immense number of *minhas Senhoras*. I had purchased a kid and a fowl, and laid down the money immediately. Persons circumstanced as they were, are sometimes robbed in a most unpardonable manner by travellers, who take advantage of their houses, eat their poultry, and leave them without paying; but considering the entire non-existence of law in these regions, I am only surprised that greater enormities are not committed.

In the afternoon we advanced as usual, and passed some deserted cottages, but toward the close of the day arrived at some that were inhabited, and at dusk put up near to two or three that stood together, after having crossed the Ceará-Mirim for the last and forty-second time.

The place at which we had arrived is reckoned to be distant forty leagues from Natal; the league of the sertão is never less than four miles, and is often much more; there are *léguas grandes*, *léguas pequenas*, and *léguas de nada*, or nothing leagues, which I have found quite long enough, notwithstanding their encouraging name. Pai Paulo may be about eight or ten leagues from Natal, which makes the *travessia* or barren crossing, thirty or thirty-two leagues. We advanced at about three miles within the hour or rather more, and travelled from half-past five to ten in the morning, and in the afternoon from two, or half-past two to six o'clock.

We had now reached again the habitations of man; there was still the same burnt-up appearance, but the wells were taken care of, the water was better, and grass, although it was dry, was still to be had. I intended to accompany the major, part of the way to his home, or the whole, but it was necessary that I should be guided by circumstances—by the accounts we heard of the state of the country; we advanced in our usual manner, resting more at midday, traversing a dead flat, and passing two or three *fazendas*, or cattle estates, each day, of which the live stock was looking very miserable, and the people half-starved.

Each cattle estate has a tolerably decent house, in which the owner or herdsman resides, and usually a few smaller habitations are scattered about upon the plain around it. The pens stand near to the principal house and enable the travellers to distinguish immediately, although at some distance, the site of a *fazenda*.

After four days, I saw that it would not be prudent to proceed farther; the accounts from the interior were bad, and we arrived at one estate, of which the cattle were all dying, and the people intending, if there was no rain very soon, to leave their houses. I now judged myself to be distant from the coast not less than two hundred miles. We had advanced northward and westward, and were therefore not far to the southward of Açu, but were to the westward of it. I now resolved to make for it, for my horses might fail, and all the country was in so bad a state that we might not have found others in a proper condition to go on with us; in fact, as I was not acting from orders, but merely for my own amusement, and as the guide was afraid of proceeding, I did not think I was authorized in persevering.

We found no change during that day, and if we had not met with a good-natured herdsman, should have fared very badly for want of water, unless we had seen some other person equally well disposed. I asked him the way to the nearest estate, which he told me and then I made inquiries about water, to which he answered, that unless I was acquainted with the place I should not find the well, and this part of our conversation ended by his turning back to show it to me regardless of thus increasing his journey four or five miles.

I may give some description of my friend, who turned back to show me the well, and this may be taken as the usual appearance of a travelling sertanejo. He rode a small horse with a long tail and mane; his saddle was rather raised before and behind; his stirrups were of rusty iron, and his bit was of the same; the reins were two very narrow thongs. His dress consisted of long pantaloons or leggings, of tanned but undressed leather, of a rusty brown color, which were tied tight round his waist, and under these are worn a pair of cotton drawers or trousers, as the seat is left unprotected by the leather. He had a tanned goatskin over his breast, which was tied behind by four strings and a jacket also made of leather, which is generally thrown over one shoulder; his hat was of the same, with a very shallow crown, and small brim; he had slipshod slippers of the same color, and iron spurs upon his naked heels— the straps of which go under the feet and prevent the risk of losing the slippers. A long whip of twisted thongs hung from his right wrist; he had a sword by his side, hanging from a belt over one shoulder; his knife was in his girdle, and his short dirty pipe in his mouth. Fastened to his saddle behind, was a piece of red baize, rolled up in the form of a great coat, and this usually contains a hammock and a change of linen—a shirt, and drawers, and perhaps a pair of nankeen pantaloons; his *boroacas* hung also on each side of the back of his saddle, and these generally contain *farinha* and dried meat on one side, and on the other a flint and steel, (dried leaves serve as tinder) tobacco, and a spare pipe. To this equipment is sometimes added a large pistol, thrust partly under the left thigh, and thus secured. The usual pace of the sertanejo's horse is a walk, approaching to a short trot; so that the horses of these people often have acquired the habit of dragging their hind legs, and throwing up the dust. The usual color of the sertanejos is a dark brown; for even those who are born white, soon become as completely tanned as the dress which they wear, from exposure to the sun.

The country I passed over from Natal never can, in any state of civilization, or from any increase of population, be rendered a fertile tract; but it might be, without doubt, much improved, if proper wells were sunk, reservoirs made for rain water, and trees planted; much might be done. The plains I crossed are of three kinds; those of which the soil is a loose sand, producing the acaju, the mangaba, and several kinds of palm or cabbage trees; upon them the grass is short, and of a kind which is not reckoned nourishing; in these situations are likewise produced several creeping plants, similar to those growing upon the common lands, near the seashore, in England, and the trees are thinly scattered. The fruit of the acaju or cashew tree and of the mangaba are most delightful, and are doubly acceptable in crossing the sands upon which they are to be met with. The former has been often described; the latter is a small round fruit, and is not unlike a crab apple in appearance, but it is sweet, and is unfit to be eaten until it drops from the tree; the pulp is fibrous and soft, and three seeds or kernels are contained in it, of which the taste approaches that of almonds. The palm or cabbage trees also afford fruits, which are eaten when other food fails; but these are insipid.

These plains are the *tabuleiros*, of which there exists also another kind, which are covered with brushwood, of stinted height, from the nature of the soil, but it is close and higher than a man on horseback. The road lies, in many places, through it; but as it does not afford any shade, and prevents the wind from alleviating the intenseness of the heat; it is here that the power of the sun is fully felt. This brushwood is, however, not too thick to prevent cattle from breaking their way through it, and feeding among it. The third description of plains are those of a better kind of soil, which produce good nourishing grass, but upon these no trees grow; small shrubs and briars alone are to be seen, and oftentimes not even these. They are, in parts, stony, and have rising ground upon them, which is not sufficiently high to deserve the name of a ridge of hills; but is enough to break the ocean-like flatness and immensity which these plains sometimes present to the traveller; after proceeding for hours, the same distance still seems to remain for him to traverse. These are the *campinas*. I passed over some spots covered with high trees, which in our own country would be called woods of considerable extent; but in Brazil, they could not be accounted of sufficient magnitude to compose a distinguishing feature in the naked regions which I traversed. The impression which a recollection of this portion of land left upon my mind is of a flat uncovered country.

We arrived at Açu on the 1st December, having travelled about 340 miles in 19 days. The continual anxiety in which I was kept, prevented me from keeping any regular journal of my proceedings.

The town of Açu is built in a square, and consists of about three hundred inhabitants; it has two churches, and a town hall and prison, at that time building; the governor was the promoter of the work. The place stands upon the great river of Açu, where it runs in two channels for a short distance; it is situated upon the northern bank of the smaller branch. There is an island of sand between the two branches, and the distance from whence the river is divided to where it is again united, is about two or perhaps three miles. We crossed their dry beds, and entered the square, which is not paved, and the sand is deep. Many of the inhabitants were at their doors, for all travellers are objects of curiosity, and our appearance increased it. I rode upon an English saddle, and this particularly attracted the notice of an equestrian people. The houses have only the ground floor; some of them are plastered, and whitewashed, but the mud of which others are composed, remains in its natural color, both within and without, and the floors also are of earth; so that in spite of the greatest care, when water is scarce, their inhabitants cannot keep themselves clean. Though the lower class of Brazilians, of all castes, have many dirty customs, allied to those of savage life, still they are remarkably clean in their persons; one of the greatest inconveniences of a situation, when a Brazilian complains of the place he happens to reside in, is the want of a river or pool of water in the neighborhood, for the purpose of bathing.

We inquired for the house of a man of color, a saddler by trade, with whom my guide was acquainted. This person, like many others, had come to his door to see the travellers; he soon recognized his friend, and came forward to speak to him. He procured a house for us during our stay; it was a small place, upon which neither plaster nor whitewash had been bestowed, with two rooms, one opening to the square, and the other to the river. When we were a little settled, and I had dressed myself, I sallied forth to visit the vicar, who resided in the best, or rather least miserable looking habitation in the town; it was about the size of the cottages of laborers, or small farmers in England, but not nearly so comfortable, though the floors were bricked.

The next day we left Açu. Our way was through

woodlands for about one league, when we came out upon the borders of the lake Piatô; we proceeded along them for another half league, and unloaded near to the *caza de palha*, or straw cottage, of the commandant of the district.

I was this afternoon surprised at a feat of dexterity of one of the commandant's sons, a boy of about fourteen years of age. I had often heard of the manner of catching the wild cattle in the sertão; the person employed for the purpose pursues on horseback, with a long pole, having a goad at one end, the animal which he is desirious of bringing to the ground, until he overtakes it—he then pierces its side between the ribs and the hip-bone, which, if it is done at the moment the beast raises its hind feet from the ground, throws it with such violence, as sometimes to make it roll over. Some oxen had often trespassed upon the commandant's maize; one of the boys could no longer bear this quietly; he therefore mounted one of his father's horses, of which there were several very fine ones, took one of the long poles and set off without a saddle, and in his shirt and drawers, to attack the animals. He drove them out of the maize, reached one of them with the goad at the right moment, and threw it down, but before he could turn his horse, another had attacked him running his horns into the fleshy part of one of the horse's thighs. The boy had taken the precaution of putting a bridle on to his horse, otherwise, if he had mounted with a halter only, he would most probably have suffered much more. One of his brothers came to his assistance, and drove the oxen quite away. The facility with which the beast was thrown proved that practice and quickness were more requisite than strength in this operation.

Early in the morning we continued our journey for some distance along the banks of the lake, and then entered upon some open land, which was now quite dry; we slept under a clump of trees, distant about twenty miles from Piatô.

The road of the next day led us through woodlands, and over loose stony ground; but the woods of this part of the country are not large and luxuriant; they have not the grandeur of the forests of Pernambuco, nor is the brushwood which grows under them so close and thick.

We continued travelling for two days over the same kind of ground; plains with trees thinly scattered, and spots of wooded land. We likewise crossed two salt-marshes; but upon these there was no mud. The water which oozes from the land, on digging into it, is salt; but the soil was dry and hard.

On the 7th December, we arrived at ten o'clock in the morning at the village of Santa Luzia, containing from two to three hundred inhabitants. It is built in a square, and has one church; the houses are small and low. Here I was able to replenish my spirit bottles, and to purchase a supply of *rapaduras*. These are cakes of brown sugar or treacle, boiled to a sufficient consistency to harden, by which means it is more portable, and much less liable to be wasted in its conveyance.

Santa Luzia stands upon the northern bank of a dry river, in a sandy loose soil. We took up our midday station under the roof of a miserable hut; the ashes of an extinguished fire in its center, and a bench of twisted twigs, alone denoted that it had served as a dwelling. Several of the inhabitants of the village soon came to us to inquire for news from Pernambuco; and among others, a young man, whose accent discovered him to be a native of some of the northern provinces of Portugal, and whose manner displayed the idea which he entertained of his own importance; he said that he had orders from the commandant to demand my passport, to which I answered that if the commandant had wished to see the passport, he would certainly have sent one of his officers to ask for it; the young man rejoined, that he was the sergeant of the district. I said that I did not doubt the truth of what he said, but that I could not know him in that capacity, because, instead of being in uniform, he had appeared in the usual dress of shirt and drawers; and I added that his manner was such that I had quite resolved not to show it to him at all. He said I must and should show it; I turned to Julio and asked him if he heard what the man said; Julio answered, "Yes, sir, never mind." The sergeant went off, and we prepared our arms much to the amazement and amusement of some of the more peaceable inhabitants. I soon saw him again, and he was coming toward us, with two or three other persons; I called to him to keep at a distance, telling him that Julio would fire if he did not. This he judged advisable to do; and as I thought it proper and prudent to advance as soon as possible, we left the place soon after one o'clock, with a broiling sun; therefore we then saw no more of the sergeant. The dry river upon which this village stands divides the captaincies of Rio Grande and Ceará, consequently there was much reason for the commandant's demand of my passport; but it was necessary to preserve the high opinion generally entertained of the name of *Inglês*, Englishman, wherever the people possessed sufficient knowledge to understand that the said *Ingleses* were not *bichos*, or animals; and also to keep up my own importance with the persons about me. It would not have answered, to have thus given way to a man who was inclined to make me feel the consequence which he judged his place would allow him to assume. If I had been invited to the commandant's house in a civil way, or if the sergeant had come to me in his uniform, all would have gone well. These trifles, though apparently of no importance, weigh very heavily with persons who had made such small advances toward civilization; public opinion is every thing. If the idea of my being a *bicho* and a heretic had not been counterbalanced by that of rank and consequence, I might have had the whole village upon me, and have been deserted by my own people into the bargain.

The general features of the captaincy of Rio Grande may be laid down as displaying tolerable fertility to the southward of Natal, and as having a barren aspect to the northward of it, excepting the banks and immediate neighborhood of the Potengi.

When I approached Aracati, I sent my Goiana guide

forward with the letter which I had received from the
governor of Rio Grande to Senhor José Fideles Barrozo, a
wealthy merchant and landed proprietor. On my arrival,
I found that the guide had delivered the letter, and that
Senhor Barrozo had given to him the keys of an unoccu-
pied house, which I was to inhabit during my stay.

The town of Aracati consists chiefly of one long street,
with several others of minor importance branching from
it to the southward; it stands upon the southern bank of
the river Jaguaribe, which is so far influenced by the tide.
At the ebb, the stream is fordable, and as it spreads considerably from the main channel, some parts remain quite
dry at low water. The houses of Aracati, unlike those of
any of the other small places which I visited, have one
story above the ground floor; I inquired the reason of this,
and was told, that the floods of the river were sometimes so
great, as to render necessary a retreat to the upper part of
the houses. The town contains three churches, and a town
hall and prison, but no monasteries; this captaincy does
not contain any such pest. The inhabitants are in number
about six hundred.

The house I was to occupy consisted of two good-
sized rooms, with large closets or small bedchambers leading from each, called *alcovas*, and a kitchen; these were all
above; and underneath there was a sort of warehouse. To
the back we had an oblong yard, enclosed by a brick wall,
with a gate at the farther end, by which our horses entered; and here they remained until better arrangements
could be made for them. I slung my hammock in the front
room, and desired that some fowls should be purchased, as
stock, while we remained here. One was preparing for me,
when three black servants appeared from Senhor Barrozo;
the first brought a large tray with a plentiful and excellent-
ly cooked supper, wine, sweetmeats, etc.; a second carried
a silver ewer and basin, and a fringed towel; and a third
came to know if there was any thing which I particularly
wished for, besides what had been prepared; this man
took back my answer, and the other two remained to at-

tend, until I had supped. I learnt from the guide afterwards that another tray had been sent for my people. I
supposed that Senhor Barrozo had thought proper to
treat me in this manner on the day of my arrival, from an
idea that I could not have arranged any means of cooking,
etc. until the next day; but in the morning coffee and cakes
were brought to me, and the same major-domo came to
know if all was to my liking. While I remained at Aracati,
Senhor Barrozo provided everything for me and for my
people, in the same handsome manner. This treatment is
usual where persons are well recommended; it is noble,
and shows the state of manners among the higher orders.

In the morning I received a visit from Senhor
Barrozo, whose manners were ceremonious and courtly.
On my mentioning the inconvenience to which I was
putting him by my stay, he said that he could not alter in
any way his mode of treating me, because, if he did, he
should not do his duty to the Governor of Rio Grande, to
whom he owed many obligations, and, consequently, took
every opportunity of showing his gratitude by all the
means in his power. The reason which he thus gave for his
civility completely set at rest any thing I could have said
to prevents its continuance.

The distance between Aracati and the Villa da
Fortaleza do Ceará Grande, is thirty leagues, principally
consisting of sandy lands covered with brushwood; in a
few places the wood is loftier and thicker, but of this there
is not much. We passed also some fine *várzeas*, or low
marshy grounds, which were now sufficiently dry for cultivation; and indeed the only land from which any crop
could be expected in this particularly severe dry season.
The country is, generally speaking, flat, and in some parts
the path led us near to the seashore, but was never upon it.
We saw several cottages, and three or four hamlets; the
facility of obtaining fish from the sea has rendered living
comparatively easy in these parts. We passed through an
Indian village, and the town of São José, each built in a
square, and each containing about three hundred inhab-

itants. I understood that the governors of Ceará are obliged
to take possession of their office at São José. We made the
journey in four days, arriving at the Villa da Fortaleza on
the 16th December, and might have entered it at noon on
the fourth day, but I preferred waiting until the evening. I
performed the journey from Natal to Ceará, a distance of
one hundred and sixty leagues, according to the vague
computation of the country, in thirty-four days. The morning after my arrival I sent back to Aracati the men and
horses which I had brought with me.

The town of the fortress of Ceará is built upon heavy
sand, in the form of a square, with four streets leading
from it, and it has an additional long street on the north
side of the square, which runs in a parallel direction, but is
unconnected with it. The dwellings have only a ground
floor, and the streets are not paved; but some of the houses
have footpaths of brick in front. It contains three churches,
the governor's palace, the town hall and prison, a customhouse, and the treasury. The number of inhabitants I
judge to be from one thousand to twelve hundred. The
fort, from which the place derives its name, stands upon a
sand hill close to the town, and consists of a sand or earth
rampart toward the sea, and of stakes driven into the
ground on the land side; it contained four or five pieces of
cannon of several sizes, which were pointed various ways;
and I observed that the gun of heaviest metal was mounted
on the land side. Those which pointed to the sea were not
of sufficient caliber to have reached a vessel in the usual
anchorage ground. The powder magazine is situated upon
another part of the sand hill, in full view of the harbor.

I rode immediately on my arrival to the house of
Senhor Marcos Antonio Briçio, the chief of the treasury
and of the naval department, with several other titles
which are not transferrable into our language; to this
gentleman I had a letter of introduction from Senhor
Barrozo. I found several persons assembled at his house to
drink tea and play at cards. Senhor Marcos is an intelli-
gent and well-informed man, who has seen good society in

Lisbon, and had held a high situation at Maranhão before he was appointed to Ceará. I was introduced to Senhor Lorenço, a merchant who had connections in trade with England; he recognized my name, for he had been acquainted with near relations of mine in Lisbon. I was invited to stay with him, and received from him every civility.

The morning after my arrival I visited the Governor, Luís Barba Alardo de Menezes, and was received by him with much affability; he said that he wished he had more opportunities of showing the regard which he entertained for my countrymen, and that some of them would come and settle in his captaincy. He built, during his administration of the province, the center of the palace, and employed Indian workmen, paying them half the usual price of labor. He was in the habit of speaking of the property of individuals residing within the province as if it was his own, saying, his ships, his cotton, etc. I happened to be at Ceará on the Queen of Portugal's birthday; the company of regular troops, consisting of one hundred and fourteen men, was reviewed; they looked respectable, and were in tolerable order. In the chief apartment of the palace stood a full-length picture of the Prince Regent of Brazil, which was placed against the wall, and was raised about three feet from the ground. Three or four steps ascended from the floor to the foot of the picture; upon the lowest of these the Governor stood in full uniform, and each person passed before him and bowed, that thus the state of the Sovereign Court might be kept up. I dined with the Governor this day, at whose table were assembled all the military and civil officers, and two or three merchants; he placed me at his right-hand, as a stranger, thus showing the estimation in which Englishmen are held. About thirty persons were present at the table, of which more than half wore uniforms; indeed the whole display was much more brilliant that I had expected; every thing was good and handsome.

I had opportunities of seeing the Indian villages of

Aronxas and Masangana, and there is a third in this neighborhood, of which I have forgotten the name; each is distant from Ceará between two and three leagues, in different directions; they are built in the form of a square, and
each contains about three hundred inhabitants. One of
my usual companions on these occasions was acquainted
with the vicar of Aronxas, and we therefore made him a
visit. He resided in a building which had formerly belonged
to the Jesuits; it is attached to the church, and has balconies from the principal corridor, which look into it.

The Indians of these villages, and indeed of all those
which I passed through, are Christians; though it is said
that some few of them follow in secret their own heathenish
rites, paying adoration to the *maracá*, and practicing all
the customs of their religion. When the Roman Catholic
religion does take root in them, it of necessity degenerates
into the most abject superstition. An adherence to super-
stitious rites, whether of Roman Catholic ordination or
prescribed by their own undefined faith, appears to be the
only part of their character in which they show any con-
stancy. Each village has its priest, who is oftentimes a vicar,
and resident for life upon the spot. A director is also attached to each village, who is supposed to be a white man;
he has great power over the persons within his jurisdiction.
If a proprietor of land is in want of workmen he applies to
the director, who agrees for the price at which the daily
labor is to be paid, and he commands one of his chief Indians to take so many men, and proceed with them to the
estate for which they are hired. The laborers receive the
money themselves, and expend it as they please; but the
bargains thus made are usually below the regular price of
labor. Each village has two *juízes ordinarios* or mayors, who
act for one year. One *juíz* is a white man, and the other an
Indian; but it may easily be supposed that the former has,
in fact, the management. These *juízes* have the power of
putting suspicious persons into confinement, and of punishing for small crimes; those of more importance wait for
the *correição*, or circuit of the *ouvidor* of the captaincy. Each

village contains a town hall and prison. The administration of justice in the sertão is generally spoken of as most wretchedly bad; every crime obtains impunity by the payment of a sum of money. An innocent person is sometimes punished through the interest of a great man, whom he may have offended, and the murderer escapes who has the good fortune to be under the protection of a powerful patron. This proceeds still more from the feudal state of the country than from the corruption of the magistrates, who might often be inclined to do their duty, and yet be aware that their exertions would be of no avail, and would possibly prove fatal to themselves. The Indians have likewise their *capitães-móres*, and this title is conferred for life; it gives the holder some power over his fellows, but as it is among them unaccompanied by the possession of property, the Indian *capitães-móres* are much ridiculed by the whites; and indeed the half-naked officer with his gold-headed cane is a personage who would excite laughter from the most rigid nerves.

The Indians are in general a quiet and inoffensive people; they have not much fidelity, but although they desert, they will not injure those whom they have served. Their lives are certainly not passed in a pleasant manner under the eye of a director, by whom they are imperiously treated; consequently it is not surprising that they should do all in their power to leave their villages, and be free from an immediate superior; but even when they have escaped from the irksome dominion of the director, they never settle in one place. The Indian scarcely ever plants for himself, or if he does, rarely waits the crop; he sells his maize or manioc for half its value, before it is fit to be gathered, and removes to some other district. His favorite pursuits are fishing and hunting; a lake or rivulet will alone induce him to be stationary for any length of time. He has a sort of independent feeling, which makes him spurn at any thing like a wish to deprive him of his own free agency; to the director he submits, because it is out of his power to resist. An Indian can never be persuaded to address the master to whom he may have hired himself, by the term of Senhor, though it is made use of by the whites in speaking to each other, and by all other free people in the country; but the Negroes also use it in speaking to their masters, therefore the Indian will not; he addresses his temporary master by the term of *amo* or *patrão*, protector or patron. The reluctance to use the term of Senhor may perhaps have commenced with the immediate descendants of those who were in slavery, and thus the objection may have become traditional. They may refuse to give by courtesy what was once required from them by law. However, if it began in this manner, it is not now continued for the same reason, as none of those with whom I conversed, and they were very many, appeared to know that their ancestors had been obliged to work as slaves.

The instances of murder committed by Indians are rare. They are pilferers rather than thieves. When they can, they eat immoderately; but if it is necessary, they can live upon a very trifling quantity of food, to which their idleness often reduces them. They are much addicted to liquor, and will dance in a ring, singing some of the monotonous ditties of their own language, and drink for nights and days without ceasing. Their dances are not indecent, as those of Africa. The mulattos consider themselves superior to the Indians, and even the créole blacks look down upon them; "he is as paltry as an Indian," is a common expression among the lower orders in Brazil. They are vilely indifferent regarding the conduct of their wives and daughters; lying and other vices attached to savage life belong to them. Affection seems to have little hold upon them; they appear to be less anxious for the life and welfare of their children than any other caste of men who inhabit that country. The women however do not, among these semi-barbarians, perform the principal drudgery; if the husband is at home, he fetches water from the rivulet and fuel from the wood; he builds the hut while his wife takes shelter in some neighbor's shed. But if they travel, she has her young children to carry, the pots, the baskets, and the excavated gourds, while the husband takes his wallet of goatskin and his hammock rolled up upon his back, his fishing net and his arms, and walks in the rear. The children are washed on the day of their birth in the nearest brook or pool of water. Both the men and the women are cleanly in many of their habits, and particularly in those relating to their persons; but in some other matters their customs are extremely disgusting; the same knife is used for all purposes and with little preparatory cleaning is employed in services of descriptions widely opposite. They do not reject any kind of food, and devour it almost without being cooked; rats and other small vermin, snakes and alligators are all accepted.

The instinct, for I know not what else to call it, which the Indians possess above other men, in finding their way across a wood to a certain spot on the opposite side without path or apparent mark, is most surprising; they trace footsteps over the dry leaves which lie scattered under the trees. The letter carriers, from one province to another, are mostly Indians, for from habit they endure great fatigue, and will walk day after day, with little rest, for months together. I have met them with their wallets made of goatskin upon their shoulders, walking at a regular pace, which is not altered by rough or smooth. Though a horse may outstrip one of these men for the first few days, still if the journey continues long, the Indian will, in the end, arrive before him. If a criminal has eluded the diligence of the police officers, Indians are sent in pursuit of him, as a last resource. It is well known that they will not take him alive; each man who sees the offender fires, for they do not wish to have any contention. Nor is it possible for the magistrate to fix upon the individual of the party who shot the criminal; for if any of them are asked who killed him, the answer invariably is, "*os homems,*" the men.

It is usually said, that a party of Indians will fight tolerably well; but that two or three will take to their heels at the first alarm. Some of them however are resolute, and sufficiently courageous; but the general character is usually supposed to be cowardly, inconstant, devoid of acute feelings, as forgetful of favors as of injuries, obstinate in trifles, regardless of matters of importance. The character of the Negro is more decided; it is worse, but it is also better. From the black race the worst of men may be formed; but they are capable likewise of great and good actions. The Indian seems to be without energy or exertion; devoid of great good or great evil. Much may at the same time be said in their favor; they have been injustly dealt with, they have been trampled upon, and afterwards treated as children; they have been always subjected to those who consider themselves their superiors, and this desire to govern them has even been carried to the direction of their domestic arrangements. But no, if they are a race of acute beings, capable of energy, of being deeply interested upon any subject, they would do more than they have done. The priesthood is open to them; but they do not take advantage of it. I never saw an Indian mechanic in any of the towns; there is no instance of a wealthy Indian; rich mulattos and Negroes are by no means rare. I have had many dealings with them as guides and carriers, and subsequently as laborers, and have no reason to complain, for I was never injured by any of them; but neither did I receive any particular good service, excepting in the instance of Julio. For guides and carriers they are well adapted, as their usual habits lead them to the rambling life which these employments encourage. As laborers, I found that they had usually a great inclination to overreach; but their schemes were badly made, and consequently easily discovered. I never could depend upon them for any length of time, and to advance money or clothing to them is a certain loss. If I had any labor which was to be performed by a given time, the overseer would always reckon upon his mulatto and Negro free people; but did not mention in the list of persons who were to work any of the Indians whom I was then employing; and on my speaking of them, he answered, "An Indian is only to be mentioned for the present day," meaning that no reliance is to be placed upon them.

Like most of the aboriginal inhabitants of the western hemisphere, these people are of a copper color. They are short, and stoutly made; but their limbs, though large, have not the appearance of possessing great strength; they have no show of muscle. The face is disproportionately broad, the nose flat, the mouth wide, the eyes deep and small, the hair black, coarse, and lank; none of the men have whiskers, and their beards are not thick. The women, when they are young, have by no means an unpleasant appearance; but they soon fall off, and become ugly; their figures are seldom well shaped. Deformity is rare among the Indians; I do not recollect to have seen an individual of this race who had been born defective; and the well-informed persons with whom I conversed were of opinion, that the Indians are more fortunate in this respect than any other race with whom they were acquainted. All the Indians of Pernambuco speak Portuguese, but few of them pronounce it well; there is always a certain twang which discovers the speaker to be an Indian, although the voice was heard without the person being seen; many of them however do not understand any other language. The Indians seldom if ever speak Portuguese so well as the generality of the creole Negroes.

It must be perfectly understood, that although there may be some unfair dealings occasionally of the director toward the Indian, still this race cannot be enslaved! the Indian cannot be made to work for any person against his inclination, he cannot be bought and sold. An Indian will sometimes make over his child, when very young, to a rich person to be taught some trade, or to be brought up as a household servant, but as soon as the child is of an age to provide for itself, it cannot be prevented from so doing; it may leave the person under whose care it has been placed if it be so inclined.

The general feature of the country about Ceará is arid; the captaincy produces no sugar, but the lands are adapted for cotton, of which however the crop this year was very trifling. So excessive had the drought become, that a famine was feared, and great distress would have been experienced if a vessel had not arrived from the southward laden with the flour of the manioc. The usual price of it was 640 *reis per alqueire*, but the cargo of this vessel was sold at 6400 *reis per alqueire*; a fact which proves the scarcity to have been very great. Formerly consider-able quantities of beef were salted and dried here, and were exported to the other captaincies, but from the mortality among the cattle, caused by the frequent dry seasons, this trade has been unavoidably given up entirely, and the whole country is now supplied from Rio Grande do Sul, the southern boundary of the Portuguese do-minions.

I was received at Ceará most hospitably; the name of Englishman was a recommendation. In the morning I generally remained at home, and in the afternoon rode out with three or four of the young men of the place, who were much superior to any I had expected to find here, and in the evening a large party usually assembled at the house of Senhor Marcos; his company and that of his wife and daughter would have been very pleasant anywhere, but was particularly so in these uncivilized regions. Parties were likewise occasionally given at the palace, and at both these places, after tea and coffee, cards and conversation made the evenings pass very quickly. The palace was the only dwelling in the town which had boarded floors: it ap-peared at first rather strange to be received by one of the principal officers of the province, in a room with a brick floor and plain whitewashed walls, as occurred at the house of Senhor Marcos.

This gentleman had delivered to me a crimson-colored red satin bag, containing government papers, and directed to the Prince Regent of Portugal and Brazil, and he gave me directions to put it into the hands of the post-master at Pernambuco. I obtained, from being the bearer, the power of requiring horses from the several comman-dants upon the road.

I had in my journey from Goiana to Ceará seen Per-nambuco, and the adjoining provinces to the northward, in almost their worst state—that of one whole season without rain; but extreme wretchedness is produced by two successive years of drought: in such a case, on the second year, the peasants die by the road side; entire families are swept away; entire districts are depopulated. The country was in this dreadful state in 1791, 2, 3, for these three years passed without any considerable fall of rain. In 1810, food was still to be purchased, though at exorbitant prices, and in the following year the rains came down in abundance, and removed the dread of famine. I had, I say, seen the provinces through which I passed upon the brink of extreme want, owing to the failure of the rains; I had myself experienced inconvenience from this cause, and in one instance considerable distress from it; now, in returning, the whole country was changed, the rains had commenced, and I was made to feel that great discomfort is caused by each extreme; but the sensations which the apprehension of a want of water produces are much more painful than the disagreeable effects of an immoderate quantity of it—heavy rains and flooded lands.

On the 8th of January, 1811, I commenced my return to Pernambuco.

VI

Life in the Sertão

I left Ceará at daybreak with three Indians, and three loaded horses, and one of the young men with whom I had formed an acquaintance accompanied me to a short distance from the town. I deviated on my return to Aracati, in some measure, from the road by which I had travelled to Ceará.

I was advised to get on to the seashore as soon as possible on leaving Aracati, this being the better road. We had had several showers of rain, occasionally for some days past, and although they were slight, the grass had begun to spring up in some places. The rapidity of vegetation in Brazil is truly astonishing. Rain in the evening, upon good soil, will by sunrise have given a greenish tinge to the earth, which is increased, if the rain continues, on the second day to sprouts of grass of an inch in length, and these on the third day are sufficiently long to be picked up by the half-starved cattle.

We advanced to the village of Santa Luzia, and rested at noon there in an unfinished cottage. Soon after we had unloaded our horses, and I had lain myself down in my hammock intending to sleep, the guide told me that a number of people appeared to be assembling near to us, and that I ought to recollect the quarrel which we had had here in going. I got up and asked for my trunk, opened it with as little apparent design as possible, turned over several things in it, and taking out the Red Bag, placed it upon a large log of timber near to me, and then I continued to search in the trunk, as if for something I could not immediately find. When I looked up again, in a few minutes, all the persons who had assembled were gone— either the important consequences attending this bag were known—that of having the power of making a requisition of horses, or some other idea of my situation in life was given by the sight of this magical bag.

On the fifth day from that of my arrival here, we set off, crossed the river, which was barely fordable, and entered upon the flooded lands. The waters covered the whole face of the country, though they were now subsiding a little. The depth was in parts up to the waist, but was in general less than knee-deep. The men knew the way from practice, but even the guide whom I had hired at Açu could not have found it without the assistance of those who carried me. At noon the hammock with me in it was hung between two trees, resting the two ends of the pole by which the men carried it upon two forked branches; and hides were placed over this pole to shade me from the sun, as the trees had not recovered from the drought, and were yet without leaves. The men slung their hammocks also, the packages were supported upon the branches of trees, and the horses stood in the water, and ate their maize out of bags which were tied round their noses.

It was seldom if ever absolutely necessary to depend upon our guns for subsistence, though the provision thus obtained was by no means unacceptable, as it varied our diet. We could generally either purchase a considerable supply of dried meat, or as occasionally occurred, it was afforded us gratuitously. Sheep were sometimes to be bought, and at others, fowls might be obtained on inquiring at the cottages; but although numbers of the latter were to be seen about the huts, and a high price offered, still the owners frequently refused to part with them. The women, naturally enough, had the management of this department of household arrangement, and after much bargaining, the housewife would often at last declare that all of them were such favorites that she and her children could not resolve to have any of them killed. This behavior became so frequent that at last when either the guide or myself rode up to a cottage to purchase a fowl, it was quite decisive with us, if the husband called to his wife, saying that she would settle the matter. Unless we had time to spare for talking, we generally went our way.

My friend the commandant was still residing at Piatô; I felt as if I was returning home; my spirits were low, and any trifle relieved them. This night I was still very unwell, my thirst was great, and nothing satisfied and allayed it so much as watermelons, of which there was here a super-abundance. I ate several of them. The guide said I should kill myself; but I thought otherwise, for I liked the fruit. In the morning I awoke quite a changed person, and the ague returned no more.

At Açu I changed one of my horses for another that was in better condition, and gave about the value of a guinea to boot. Our friends, the saddler and the owner of the house which we had inhabited in going, received us very cordially, and offered to assist us in crossing the river, which was full; but they advised me to wait for a decrease of the depth and rapidity of the stream; however I was anxious to advance, and my people made no objection. Here I discharged the young man whom I had taken from hence as a guide to Aracati. We crossed the smaller branch of the river with the water reaching to the flaps of the saddles. When we arrived at the second and principal branch, it was discovered that a *jangada* would be neces-sary to convey the baggage across. Several of the inhabi-tants of the place had followed us, judging that this would be the case, and they were willing to be of service to us in expectation of being compensated for their trouble. A few logs of timber were soon procured; the cords with which the packages were fastened to the packsaddles were made use of to tie the logs together, for the purpose of forming the raft. When the raft was prepared, the saddles and all the packages were placed upon it, and I sat down among them. Four men laid hold of each side of the raft, and shoved off from the shore, and when they lost their footing, each man kept hold of the raft with one hand, swimming with the other; but notwithstanding their exertions, the stream carried us down about fifty yards before we reached the other side, which however was gained in safety. The

Indians were already there with the horses.

January is not, properly speaking, the rainy season. The rains at the commencement of the year are called the *primeiras águas* or the first waters, and continue for about a fortnight or three weeks, after which the weather generally becomes again settled until May or June, and from this time until the end of August the rains are usually pretty constant. From August or September until the opening of the year there is not usually any rain. The dry weather can be depended upon with more certainty from September until January, than from February until May; likewise the wet weather can be looked for with more certainty from June until August than in January. There are very few days during the whole course of the year of incessant rain. What I have said regarding the seasons must however be taken with some latitude, as in all climates they are subject to variation.

I had now left the sertão, and though it treated me rather roughly, still I have always wished I could have seen more of it. There is a certain pleasure which I cannot describe in crossing new countries, and that portion of territory over which I had travelled was new to an Englishman.

Unlike the peons of the country in the vicinity of the river Plata, the sertanejo has about him his wife and family, and lives in comparative comfort. The cottages are small and are built of mud, but afford quite sufficient shelter in so fine a climate; they are covered with tiles where these are to be had, or, as is more general, with the leaves of the carnaúba. Hammocks usually supply the place of beds, and are by far more comfortable, and these are likewise frequently used as chairs. Most of the better sort of cottages contain a table, but the usual practice is for the family to squat down upon a mat in a circle, with the bowls, dishes, or gourds in the center, thus to eat their meals upon the floor. Knives and forks are not much known, and are not at all made use of by the lower orders. It is the custom in every house, from the highest to the

lowest, as in former times, and indeed the same practice
prevails in all the parts of the country which I visited, for
a silver basin, or one of earthenware, or a *cuia*, and a
fringed cambric towel, or one that is made of the coarse
cotton cloth of the country, to be handed round, that all
those who are going to sit down to eat may wash their
hands; and the same ceremony takes place again after the
meal is finished. Of the gourds great use is made in domestic arrangements; they are cut in two, and the pulp is
scooped out, then the rind is dried, and these rude vessels
serve almost every purpose of earthenware—water is carried in them, etc. and they are likewise used as measures.
They vary from six inches in circumference to about three
feet, and are usually rather of an oval shape. The gourd
when whole is called *cabaça*, and the half of the rind is
called *cuia*. It is a creeping plant, and grows spontaneously
in many parts, but in others the people plant it among the
manioc.

The conversation of the sertanejos usually turns upon
the state of their cattle or of women, and, occasionally,
accounts of adventures which took place at Recife or at
some other town. The merits or demerits of the priests
with whom they may happen to be acquainted are likewise discussed, and their irregular practices are made a
subject of ridicule. The dress of the men has already been
described, but when they are at home a shirt and drawers
alone remain. The women have a more slovenly look, as
their only dress is a shift and petticoat, no stockings, and
oftentimes no shoes; but when they leave home, which is
very seldom, an addition is made of a large piece of coarse
white cloth, either of their own or of European manufacture, and this is thrown over the head and shoulders; a
pair of shoes is likewise then put on. They are good horse-
women, and the high Portuguese saddle serves the purpose of a sidesaddle very completely. I never saw any Brazilian woman riding, as is the case occasionally in Portugal,
in the manner that men do. Their employment consists in
household arrangements entirely, for the men even milk

the cows and goats: the women spin and work with the needle. No females of free birth are ever seen employed in any kind of labor in the open air, excepting in that of occasionally fetching wood or water, if the men are not at home. The children generally run about naked until a certain age, but this is often seen even in Recife; to the age of six or seven years, boys are allowed to run about without any clothing. Formerly, I mean before the commencement of a direct trade with England, both sexes dressed in the coarse cotton cloth which is made in the country; the petticoats of this cloth were sometimes tinged with a red dye, which was obtained from the bark of the *cuipuna* tree, a native of their woods; and even now this dye is used for tinging fishing nets, as it is said that those which have undergone this process last longer.

In those times, a dress of the common printed cotton of English or of Portuguese manufacture cost from eight to twelve *mil reis*, from two to three guineas, owing to the monopoly of the trade, by which the merchants of Recife put what price they pleased upon their commodities; other things were in proportion. Owing to the enormous prices, European articles of dress could of course only be possessed by the rich people. However, since the opening of the ports to foreign trade, English goods are finding their way all over the country, and the hawkers are now a numerous body of men.

The women seldom appear, and when they are seen do not take any part in the conversation, unless it be some one good wife who rules the roost; if they are present at all when the men are talking, they stand or squat down upon the ground, in the doorway leading to the interior of the house, and merely listen. The morals of the men are by no means strict, and when this is the case, it must give an unfavorable bias, in some degree, to those of the women; but the sertanejo is very jealous, and more murders are committed, and more quarrels entered into on this score, by ten-fold, than on any other. These people are revengeful; an offence is seldom pardoned, and in default of law, of which there is scarcely any, each man takes it into his own hands. Robbery in the sertão is scarcely known; the land is in favorable years too plentiful to afford temptation, and in seasons of distress for food, every man is for the most part equally in want. Subsistence is to be obtained in an easier manner than by stealing in so abundant a country, and where both parties are equally brave and resolute; but besides these reasons, I think the sertanejos are a good race of people. They are tractable, and might easily be instructed, excepting in religious matters; in these they are fast rivetted; and such was their idea of an Englishman and a heretic, that it was on some occasions difficult to make them believe that I, who had the figure of a human being, could possibly belong to that nondescript race. They are extremely ignorant, few of them possessing even the commonest rudiments of knowledge. Their religion is confined to the observance of certain forms and ceremonies, and to the frequent repetition of a few prayers, faith in charms, relics, and other things of the same order. The sertanejos are courageous, generous, sincere, and hospitable: if a favor is begged, they know not how to deny it; but if you trade with them either for cattle, or aught else, the character changes, and then they wish to outwit you, conceiving success to be a piece of cleverness of which they may boast.

The color of the sertanejos varies from white, of which there are necessarily few, to a dark brown; the shades of which are almost as various as there are persons: two of exactly the same tint are scarcely to be met with. Children of the same parents rarely if ever are of the same shade; some difference is almost always perceivable, and this is, in many instances, so glaring, as to lead at first to doubts of the authenticity; but it is too general to be aught but what is right. The sertanejo, if color is set aside, is certainly handsome; and the women, while young, have well-shaped forms, and many of them good features; indeed I have seen some of the white persons who would be admired in any country. Their constant exposure to the sun, and its great power at a distance from the sea, darkens the complexion more than if the same persons had resided upon the coast; but this gives them a decided dark color, which has the appearance of durability, and is much preferable to a sallow sickly look, though of a lighter tint.

The persons who reside upon and have the care of the cattle estates, are called *vaqueiros*, which simply means cowherds. They have a share of the calves and foals that are reared upon the land, but of the lambs, pigs, goats, etc. no account is given to the owner; and from the quantity of cattle, numbers are reckoned very loosely; it is therefore a comfortable and lucrative place, but the duties attending it are heavy, require considerable courage, and great bodily strength and activity. Some of the owners live upon their estates; but the major part of those through which I passed, were possessed by men of large property, who resided in the towns upon the coast, or who were at the same time sugar planters.

The interior of Pernambuco, Rio Grande, Paraíba, and Ceará contains, properly speaking, no wild cattle. Twice every year the herdsmen from several estates assemble for the purpose of collecting the cattle. The cows are driven from all quarters into the area in front of the house, and here, surrounded by several horsemen, are put into spacious pens. This being done, the men dismount, and now their object is, if any of the cows are inclined to be unruly, which is often the case, to noose them by the horns so as to secure them; or another mode is adopted, which is by noosing one of the hind-legs, and carrying the cord quite round the animal, so as to throw it down. The calves are then caught, and this is done without much difficulty; they are marked on the right haunch with a red-hot iron, which is made of the shape that has been fixed upon by the owner as his peculiar mark.

When the oxen are to be collected for a market, the service is more dangerous, and frequently the rider is under the necessity of throwing the animal to the ground with his long pole. On the man's approach, the ox runs off into the nearest wood, and the man follows, as closely as he possibly can, that he may take advantage of the opening of the branches which is made by the beast, as these shortly close again, resuming their former situation. At times the ox passes under a low and thick branch of a large tree, then the man likewise passes under the branch, and that he may do this, he leans to the right side so completely, as to enable him to lay hold of the girth of his saddle with his left hand, and at the same time his left heel catches the flap of the saddle; thus with the pole in his right hand, almost trailing upon the ground, he follows without slackening his pace, and being clear of this obstacle, again resumes his seat. If he can overtake the ox, he runs his goad into its side, and if this is dexterously done, he throws it. Then he dismounts, and ties the animal's legs together, or places one fore-leg over one of the horns, which secures it most effectually. Many blows are received by these men, but it is seldom that deaths are occasioned.

When a traveller is in distress for water, he cannot do better than to follow the first cattle path, as these usually lead to the nearest pool of water, in a direct line. The paths are easily distinguished, being very narrow, and the wood uniting above, leaving open below only a shady walk, of the height of the animals which made it.

Each lot of mares with its master horse is driven into the pens; this consists of from fifteen to twenty in number. The foals are likewise marked in the same manner as the calves. It is worthy of remark, and the circumstance was often repeated to me, that the horse of the lot drives from it not only the colts but the fillies also, as soon as they are full grown. The fact was only qualified in two or three instances, when told to me, by the person who related it adding, that if the horse did not do so, he was taken from the lot, and broken for the packsaddle, being considered of a bad breed.

When a horse is to be tamed for any purpose whatsoever, he is noosed, after being put into a pen, and is tied to a stake; on the following day, or perhaps the same afternoon, if he appears at all tractable, a small low saddle is placed upon him, and a man then mounts with a double halter. The animal runs off with him, which the man, far from attempting to prevent, rather urges him to do; though in general the whip and spur are not made use of, unless he is obstinate and refuses to go forward. Horses of good breeds are said to be those most easily tamed. The horse runs until he becomes weary, and is then brought back quietly by its rider; and perhaps they do not reach the rider's home until the following day. The man must not dismount until he has returned to the spot from whence he started, as he would probably experience great difficulty when he wished again to proceed, from the restiveness of the horse. The same operation is continued as long as the animal is not supposed to be effectually broken in, and safe to mount. It happens on some occasions, that, by plunging, the horse gets rid of both man and saddle, and is not again seen for a length of time; however, unless the girths give way, he has little chance of throwing his rider, for the sertanejos are most excellent horsemen.

The horses are small, and some of them are finely shaped, though little attention is paid to the improvement of the breed. Great stress is laid upon the color, in the choice of these animals; some colors being accounted more demonstrative of strength than others. Thus a cream-colored horse, with a tail and mane of the same color, is rejected for the packsaddle, or for any kind of severe labor; and if horses of this description are sold for these purposes, the price is lower than that of an animal of an equally promising appearance in form and size, of any other tinge: they are much esteemed if well shaped, as saddle-horses, for short distances. A cream-colored horse, with a black tail and mane, is reckoned strong. The horses that have one fore-leg white, and the other of the color of the body, are supposed to be liable to stumble. The usual colors are bay and gray; but chestnut, black, and cream-color are less common; those most esteemed for work are dark bays, with black tails and manes, and grays dotted with small bay spots. Stallions are broken in both for the saddle and for carrying loads in the neighborhood of the towns; but the sertanejos, both from necessity and from their knowledge of their superior ability to perform hard labor, make use of geldings. It is not always safe to ride a high-spirited horse in the sertão, because when he begins to neigh, instances have occurred of some master horse coming to give him battle, and as both are equally desirous of fighting, the rider may perhaps find himself under the necessity of placing himself at a distance from the combatants. However, if he should chance to have a good stick in his hand, and can prevent his own horse from rearing as the wild horse approaches, he may come off in safety.

Sheep are kept upon every estate for their flesh, when that of a more esteemed kind fails; that is, either when the oxen are in a meager state, owing to a long continuance of dry weather; or that the herdsman is too much occupied at home, or too lazy to go out and kill one. The mutton is never well-tasted, and though it is true that in the sertão no care whatever is taken in rearing or feeding the sheep, still I do not think that this kind of meat is to be brought to any great perfection. The lambs are covered with fine wool, and this continues until they are one year and a half or two years old; but after this age, it begins to drop, and is replaced by a species of hair. Although the wool should remain longer in some instances, it appeared to me that it was coarse and short.

The division of property in the sertão is very undeterminate, and this may be imagined, when I say that the common mode of defining the size of a *fazenda* is by computing it at so many leagues; or, as in some cases, by so many hundreds of calves yearly, without any reference to the quantity of land. Few persons take the trouble of making themselves acquainted with the exact extent of their own property, and perhaps could not discover it if they made the attempt.

The climate is good; indeed the inland flat country is much more healthy than that immediately bordering the coast. I can hardly name any disorders that appear to be peculiar to it; but several are known. Agues are not common, but they exist. Dropsy also they are acquainted with. Ulcers in the legs are common, but less so than upon the coast. Ruptures frequently occur. The smallpox makes dreadful ravages, and the measles are much dreaded. When the veneral disease has once settled, the sufferer seldom gets rid of it entirely; applications of herbs are used, but as these people are unacquainted with or unable to follow its proper mode of treatment, some of the patients are crippled, and the major part of them never again enjoy good health. The yaws also is to be met with. Instances of consumption occur. The whooping cough did not appear to be known in any part of the country which I visited. I slept many times in the open air, and never felt any bad effects from so doing. The dew is trifling, and a high wind is usual in the night. The sun is powerful, and is of course particularly felt in travelling over sandy loose soil; but it did not seem to do any mischief. I never suffered from headache, and, excepting the attack of the ague, which is accounted for from the heavy rain which we experienced, I never enjoyed better health.

The food of the inhabitants of the sertão consists chiefly of meat, of which they make three meals; and to this is added the flour of the manioc stirred up into paste, or rice sometimes supplies its place. The bean, which is commonly called in England the French bean, is a favorite food; it is suffered to run to seed, and is only plucked up when quite dry and hard. I have often been surprised to see of how little service maize is to them as food, but yet it is occasionally used. In default of these, the paste of the carnaúba is made; and I have seen meat eaten with curds. Of green vegetables they know nothing, and they laugh at the idea of eating any kind of salad. The wild fruits are numerous, and to be obtained in any quantities, but few species are cultivated; among the latter are the watermelon and the plantain. The cheese of the sertão, when it is fresh, is excellent; but after four or five weeks, it becomes

hard and tough. In the towns even of the sertão, rancid
Irish butter is the only kind which is to be obtained.
Wherever the lands admit of it, these people plant manioc,
rice, etc. but much, I may say the greater part of the vegetable portion of their food, is brought either from more
fertile districts near to the coast, or from the settlements
still further back—the valleys and skirts of the Cariris,
Serra do Teixeira, and other inland mountains.

The trade of the sertão consists in receiving small
quantities of European manufactured goods; the cotton
cloth of the country, of which they make some among
themselves; a small portion of European white earthenware, and considerable quantities of the dark brown ware
of the country, which is made for the most part by the Indians who live in the districts that contain the proper kind
of clay; rum in small casks; butter, tobacco, snuff, sugar
or treacle made up in cakes, spurs, bits for bridles, and
other gear for their horses, excepting the saddles, of which
the greater part are made in their own districts; gold and
silver ornaments also find a market to a certain amount.
The peddlers travel about from village to village, and from
one estate to another, bartering their commodities for
cattle of all kinds, cheese, and hides of horned cattle. A colt
of from two to three years sells for about one guinea; a
horse broken in for the packsaddle, for two or three guineas;
a horse broken in for mounting, from five to six guineas. A
bullock of two years, ten shillings; a full grown ox, one
guinea and a half; a cow varies much, according to the
quantity of milk, from one guinea to five guineas. A sheep,
from two to three shillings; a goat for slaughter is worth
even less, but a good milch goat is valued at one guinea,
and sometimes higher. Children are frequently suckled by
goats, which increases the value of these animals. The goat
that has been so employed always obtains the name of
comadre, the term which is made use of between the
mother and godmother of a child; and so general is this,
that she-goats are frequently called *comadres*, without having had the honor of suckling a young master or mistress.

Dogs are sometimes valued at from one to two guineas, and even higher, if they are good sporting, or good house and baggage dogs. A fowl is as dear as a sheep or goat; and in one instance I paid four times the money for one of these birds that I had given for a kid. The hawkers seldom obtain money in exchange for their wares; they take whatever is offered, and hire people to assist in conveying the cattle or produce to a market, where they are exchanged for goods, and then the owner again returns. A twelve-month is sometimes passed in turning over the property once; but the profits are usually enormous, two or three hundred per cent.

I had arranged that I should leave Natal in the morning of the 6th February. I passed again through São José, the Indian village, but did not turn off from the road toward Papari. I slept at a hamlet, and in the morning proceeded to Cunhà û. The next day we passed some sugar plantations and over some hills; the country was most beautiful, for everything looked green and healthy.

I crossed a considerable rivulet at the foot of a hill, and, ascending on the opposite side, put up at a single cottage, which was inhabited by white people; an old man, a widower, with a fine family of handsome sons and daughters. Their cottage had not room for us all, and therefore we intended to sleep in the open air altogether, but the old man insisted upon my going to sleep in the house, and I was not sorry for this, being rather afraid of a return of the ague. Nearly at sunset, or at the close of the day, which in that country are almost about the same time, the tame sheep was missing; great search was made for it, but to no purpose. The old man ordered two of his sons to set out, and not to return until every inquiry had been made in the neighborhood. I did all in my power to prevent giving this trouble, but he persisted, saying, "No, you are under my roof and this unfortunate circumstance may lead you to have an unfavorable opinion of me." Long after dark the young men returned with the sheep and a mulatto man in custody. I wished the man to be released, but they said that this could not be, for he was a runaway slave who had committed many depredations, and for whose apprehension a considerable reward was offered by his master.

Our journey took us again through the village of Mamanguape; and a little distance beyond it, I left the road, accompanied by the guide, and went to the principal house of a sugar plantation, where we asked for a night's lodging. I was told that the master was not at home, and great doubts seemed to be entertained of taking us in. While we were talking at the door, a young man of dark color came up, mounted a horse which was standing there without a saddle, and rode off, seemingly avoiding to observe that there were any strangers present. One of the black women said, "Why did not you speak to him, for he is one of our young masters." I now inquired and discovered that the owner of the place and his family were mulattos. This was the only instance of incivility I met with, and the only occasion on which a night's lodging was denied to me during the whole course of my stay in Brazil.

Toward the evening of the following day we reached a hamlet, and at one of the cottages I obtained permission to pass the night. There was a penthouse standing out from the front; these are usual even for dwellings of wealthy persons. Under it I slung my hammock, but was surprised to find, that though the house was inhabited, still the door was shut, and that the person within spoke to us, but did not open it. This I thought strange, and began to suppose that he might be afflicted with some contagious disorder, and had been forsaken by his friends, or rather, that his family had been advised to remove to some neighboring cottage. But the guide explained, saying that the man had been bitten by a snake, and that the bite of this species only became fatal if the man who had received it saw any female animal, and particularly a woman, for thirty days after the misfortune. As the lower orders imagine that all snakes are poisonous, it is not surprising that many remedies or charms should be quoted as efficacious. It is well known that many of those reptiles are innoxious, but this is not believed by the people in general.

On the morrow we left these good people in expectation of their friend's restoration to health at the allotted period, and proceeded to dine on the banks of the river Paraíba, at a spot which was not far distant from the plantation of Espirito Santo, where we had slept on our way northward. We arrived upon the banks about ten o'clock, and heard from several persons of a report which had been spread, that the river was filling fast. About twelve o'clock the water made its appearance, and before we left it the river was three feet deep. We afterward heard that the stream was not fordable at five o'clock of the same afternoon, and that it continued to run with great rapidity for some days.

I was received by my friends at Goiana in their usual friendly manner; but I found that the town was in a dreadful state from the scarcity of provisions. One person was said to have died of hunger, and I was told by an inhabitant that several respectable women had been at his house to beg for *farinha*, offering to pawn their gold ornaments for it.

On the morning of the 15th February, I left Goiana, and assisted my people in crossing the river. As soon as they were all safe on the Recife side of it, I pushed on accompanied by Julio and Feliciano, all three of us being mounted upon our best horses. We rested during the heat of the day at Igaraçu. My horse recognized the place, for as he entered the town, he quickened his pace, and without being guided, went up to the door of the inn, from whence he refused to stir again until I dismounted. We arrived a little after sunset at the Cruz das Almas. John was prepared for me, but did not expect me for one or two days.

The following morning I rode to Recife, and was received by my friends as one who had been somewhat despaired of.

VII

MARANHÃO

Eight days after my return from Ceará arrived a vessel
from England, bringing letters which obliged me to leave
Pernambuco and proceed to Maranhão. As a cargo could
not be obtained for the brig at the former place, the consignee determined to send her to Maranhão, and being
myself desirious of taking advantage of the first opportunity, I prepared for the voyage, and sailed in the course of
forty-eight hours.

We weighed anchor on the 25th February, and had a
prosperous passage of seven days. We were in sight of the
land nearly the whole time, and occasionally, as the brig
was small, and the master wished, if possible, to become
acquainted with the points of land, we were very near to it.

As the brig came up the harbor, we received the
health and customhouse visit. It was composed of several
well-dressed men, some of whom wore cocked hats and
swords; and all of them ate much bread and cheese, and
drank quantities of porter. The *administrador* of the customs was among them, and was dressed in the uniform of
a cavalry officer. I scarcely ever saw so much astonishment
pictured in the countenance of any man as in that of the
master of the brig. He had been accustomed to enter our
own ports, where so much business is done in so quiet a
manner; and he now said to me in half joke, half earnest,
"Why it is not only one, but they are coming in shoals to
take the ship from me." After all these personages, and all
the trouble they had given us, I was still obliged to pass the
night on board, because the *guardamor*, the officer especially
appointed to prevent smuggling, had not made his visit.

The city of São Luís, situated upon the island of
Maranhão, and the metropolis of the *estado*, or state of
Maranhão, is the residence of a captain-general and the

see of a bishop. It is built upon very unequal ground, commencing from the water's edge, and extending to the distance of about one mile and a half in a NE direction. The space which it covers ought to contain many more inhabitants than is actually the case; but the city is built in a straggling manner, and it comprises some broad streets and squares. This gives to it an airy appearance, which is particularly pleasant in so warm a climate. Its situation upon the western part of the island, and upon one side of a creek, almost excludes it from the sea breeze, by which means the place is rendered less healthy than if it was more exposed. The population may be computed at about 12,000 persons or more, including Negroes, of which the proportion is great, being much more considerable than at Pernambuco. The streets are mostly paved, but are out of repair. The houses are many of them neat and pretty, and of one story in height; the lower part of them is appropriated to the servants, to shops without windows, to warehouses, and other purposes, as at Pernambuco. The family lives upon the upper story, and the windows of this reach down to the floor, and are ornamented with iron balconies. The churches are numerous, and there are likewise Franciscan, Carmelite and other convents. The places of worship are gaudily decorated in the inside; but no plan of architecture is aimed at in the formation of the buildings themselves, with the exception of the convents, which preserve the regular features appertaining to such edifices. The governor's palace stands upon rising ground, not far from the water-side, with the front toward the town. It is a long uniform stone building, of one story in height; the principal entrance is wide, but without a portico. The western end joins the town hall and prison, which appear to be part of the same edifice; and the oblong piece of ground in its front, covered with grass, gives to it on the whole a handsome and striking appearance. One end of this is open to the harbor and to a fort in the hollow, close to the water; the other extremity is nearly closed by the cathedral. One side is almost taken up with the palace and other public buildings, and the opposite space is occupied by dwelling houses and streets leading down into other parts of the city. The ground upon which the whole place stands is composed of a soft red stone; so that the smaller streets leading from the town into the country, some of which are not paved, are full of gullies, through which the water runs in the rainy season. These streets are formed of houses consisting only of the ground floor, and having thatched roofs; the windows are without glass, and the dwellings have a most mean and shabby appearance. The city contains a customhouse and treasury; the former is small, but was quite large enough for the business of the place, until lately.

The harbor is formed by a creek in the island, and is to be entered from the Bay of São Marcos. The channel is of sufficient depth for common-sized merchant ships; but is very narrow, and not to be entered without a pilot. The Bay of São Marcos is spotted with several beautiful islands, and is of sufficient extent to admit of considerable grandeur. The width from São Luís to the opposite shore is between four and five leagues; its length is much greater; toward the south end there are several sandbanks, and the water is shallower.

The importance of the province has increased very rapidly. Previous to the last sixty years no cotton was exported, and I heard that when the first parcel was about to be shipped, a petition was made by several of the inhabitants to the *cámara* or municipality, requesting that the exportation might not be permitted, for otherwise they feared that there would be a want of the article for the consumption of the country; this of course was not attended to, and now the number of bags exported annually is between forty and fifty thousand, averaging about 180 lbs. weight each. The quantity of rice grown there is likewise great; but the sugar which is required for the consumption of the province is brought from the ports to the southward. Some sugar cane has lately been planted, but hitherto molasses only have been made. I heard many persons say that the lands are not adapted to the growth of the sugar cane. The cotton and rice are brought to São Luís in barks of about 25 or 30 tons burden. These come down the rivers with the stream from the plantations; their return is not however so easy, as they are obliged to be rowed or warped, but being then empty, or nearly so, the difficulty is not very great.

Considerable quantities of manufactured goods have been sent out from Great Britain since the opening of the trade, as has been done to the other principal ports upon the coast; but a ready sale has not been found for them here to any great amount. The province of Maranhão will not bear comparison with that of Pernambuco. It is still in an infant state; there still exist wild Indians, and the plantations upon the main land are still in danger from their attacks. The proportion of free persons is much smaller; the slaves very much preponderate, but this class can of necessity use but little of what is in any degree expensive, of what in such a climate is mere luxury. There exists at São Luís a great inequality of ranks; the chief riches of the place are in the hands of a few men who possess landed property to a great extent, numerous gangs of slaves, and are also merchants. The wealth of these persons and the characters of some of the individuals who enjoy it have raised them to great weight and consequence, and indeed one governor knows to his cost that without their concurrence it was useless to attempt the introduction of the innovations proposed, and impossible to trample long upon the rest of the community. But the great inequality of rank bespeaks the advancement of this place to have been less rapid than that of other settlements further south, where the society is more amalgamated, and property more divided. As a port of trade with Europe, São Luís may be accounted the fourth establishment upon the coast of Brazil in point of importance, giving precedence to Rio de Janeiro, Baía, and Pernambuco.

I soon discovered that São Luís was ruled with most despotic sway; the people were afraid of speaking, as no man knew how soon it might be his fate to be arrested, from some trifling expression which he might allow to escape him. The governor was so tenacious of the honors due to his situation that he required every person who crossed the area in front of the palace to remain uncovered until he had entirely passed the whole building. Not that the governor was himself always in view, but this adoration was thought necessary even to the building within which he dwelt. The distinction, until then reserved by the Romish church for its highest dignitaries, was however not thought by His Excellency too exalted for himself; the bells of the cathedral rang every time he went out in his carriage. Persons, even of the first rank in the place, were to stop, if in their carriages or on horseback, when they met him, and were to allow him to pass before they were again to move forward.

The governor was a very young man, and a member of one of the first noble families of Portugal. There are few situations in which it is so greatly in a man's power to be much beloved or much disliked as that of governor of a province in Brazil; in which a man may be either the benefactor or the scourge of the people over whom he is sent to rule.

My friend's residence, in which I stayed during my visit to Maranhão, was situated by the water-side, and almost within hail of the ships at anchor in the harbor. I was amused sometimes at the rapidity with which the fishermen paddled their canoes; these are long, and of just width sufficient to allow of two men sitting abreast. I have seen in one of them as many as sixteen men in two rows, with each a paddle, which they move with quickness and great regularity. The last men upon the bench steer the canoe when necessary, placing the paddle so as to answer the purpose of a rudder; one or other of the two men steering, according to the direction which the vessel is to take. These fellows are mostly dark-colored mulattos and blacks, and are entirely naked excepting the hats which they wear upon their heads; but when they come on shore, they partially clothe themselves. The nakedness of the Negro slaves is also not sufficiently concealed; neither males nor females have any covering from the waist upward, excepting on Sundays and holidays. I speak here of slaves who are at work in the streets, for the household servants are at least tolerably covered, and some of them are neatly and even gaudily dressed. At Pernambuco, the slaves are always decently clothed. The criminals who are to be seen chained together, as at Pernambuco, are here more numerous; and in walking the streets, the clanking of the chains is continually striking the ear, reminding every man of the state of the government under which he resides. Such is the power of a governor, that a respectable person might be sentenced to this dreadful punishment, at least until redress could be obtained from the seat of the supreme government at Rio de Janeiro, a period of four months or more intervening.

I brought with me the horse which had carried me as far as Rio Grande on my journey to Ceará, and took several rides in the neighborhood of the city, with an English gentleman who was residing there. The roads are extremely bad, even in the immediate vicinity of São Luís, and our usual practice was to ride several times round the open piece of ground upon which the barracks stand. Maranhão is again in this respect far behind the place I had lately left; the number of country houses is small; the paths are few, and no care is taken of them. Notwithstanding this, several persons have carriages, which are of a form similar to those used in Lisbon, and not unlike the cabriolets drawn by a pair of horses, which are to be seen in France and Flanders. The horses that may be purchased at São Luís are small, and few of them are well formed. Grass is scarce, and the inducements to take exercise on horseback are so few that the number of these animals upon the island is not considerable; this, too, may be one cause why fine horses are not to be met with there; for if a ready sale was found for the beasts of this description, some would, doubtless, be carried from Piauí to Maranhão, which might be done with almost as little difficulty as is experienced in conveying many of them from the interior of Pernambuco to Recife.

I nearly lost a number of books which I had brought with me; the box containing them was carried to the customhouse; they were taken out, and I was desired to translate each title page, which I did. Though the works were chiefly historical, still I found that the officer who looked over them was not inclined to let me have them, and a hint was given to me by one of my acquaintance that they might be considered as irrecoverable; however I made immediately a petition to the governor, to be allowed to send them on board again; this was granted, and thus I regained possession. If I had delayed, I am almost certain that I should not have seen them again. Such are the difficulties which are experienced with books in the parts of Brazil which I visited, that the only resource which remains is that of smuggling them into the country.

I brought a letter from one of my acquaintance at Pernambuco to a gentleman who resided at Alcântara, a town on the opposite side of the bay of São Marcos. My friend at São Luís, another young Portuguese, and myself, accompanied by two servants, agreed to hire a vessel and go over, for the purpose of making him a visit, and of seeing the place. We hired a small bark, and set sail one morning early, with a fair but light wind. The beauties of the bay are only to be seen in crossing it; the number of islands diversify the view every five minutes, from the discovery of some hidden point, or from a change in the form of the land, owing to the progress of the boat. The entrance into the harbor of Alcântara, the town itself, and the size of the vessel in which we were, reminded me much of the models of these realities. The town is built upon a semicircular hill, and at first sight from the port is very pretty; but it falls short of its promise on a nearer examination.

The evening we passed with our new friend and his partner, both of whom were pleasant men. The latter took us to a neighboring church, to hear a famous preacher, and to see all the fashion and beauty of the place. It was much crowded, and therefore we saw little or nothing of the congregation; but the preacher, a large handsome Franciscan friar, with a fine-toned and clear voice, delivered a very florid discourse, with much energy and animation. This man and one other were the only persons of those I heard preach in Brazil, who deviated from the common praises usually given to the Virgin and to the saints. It was a good practical sermon, inculcating moral duties.

I was introduced by my friend to a respectable family of São Luís. We made them a visit one evening without invitation as is the custom, and were ushered into a tolerably-sized room, furnished with a large bed, and three handsomely worked hammocks, which were slung across in different directions; there were likewise in the apartment a chest of drawers and several chairs. The mistress of the house, an elderly lady, was seated in a hammock, and a female visitor in another, but her two daughters and some male relations sat upon chairs. The company, which consisted of two or three men besides ourselves, formed a semicircle toward the hammocks. There was much ceremony, and the conversation was carried on chiefly by the men, and an occasional remark was made by one or other of the old ladies. An answer was given by the daughters to a question asked, but no more, and some of the subjects touched upon would not have been tolerated in mixed society in England. A part of the formality might perhaps have worn off on further acquaintance. The education, however, of women is not attended to, which of necessity curtails the possibility of their entering into conversation upon many subjects, even if so to do was accounted proper. Still the ladies of São Luís cannot be said to be generally thus reserved, for gaming among both sexes is much practiced, and is carried to great excess.

Two English merchants only were established at São Luís; the commercial transactions of British houses of trade were intrusted chiefly to Portuguese merchants of the place. Many of these were accustomed to little ceremony, and walked the streets in short jackets, some of them were without neckcloths and a few without stockings; but others dressed according to the manner of persons in Europe. It was with much difficulty that I could persuade the generality of those with whom I conversed that I had no business to transact; they could not comprehend the motive by which a man could be actuated who was putting himself, by travelling, to certain inconveniences for the sake of amusement; indeed many persons would not be convinced, and thought that in so saying I had some sinister views.

As it was my intention to pass the ensuing summer in England, and no ships arrived from thence, I was afraid of being delayed some months for a conveyance, therefore I thought it better to take my passage in one of the ships which were about to sail. I preferred the "Brutus," as I was intimate with the supercargo, a young Portuguese. We set sail from São Luís on the 8th of April. We arrived safe off Falmouth on the 20th of May. Here the supercargo and myself landed, and proceeded to London.

VIII

CHANGING RECIFE AND A TOUR WITH A CAPITÃO-MOR

At the commencement of the winter my friends again recommended a return to a more temperate climate than that of England; and therefore understanding that the Portuguese ship "Serra Pequeno" was upon the point of sailing, I took my passage in her. She was lying at Gravesend, and on the 4th of October, 1811, I embarked again for Pernambuco.

Contrary winds detained the ship at Portsmouth for about six weeks. On the 20th November, the wind came round to the northward and eastward, and the signal guns from the ships of war, appointed as convoys, awakened us.

The "Serra Pequeno" is one of the heavy deep-waisted Brazil ships, requiring a great number of hands to manage her. The business of the ship was carried on in a manner similar in almost all points to that which is practiced on board of British merchant vessels; there was however less cleanliness observed, and more noise was made. The second officer, who is called in the British merchant service the mate, bears in Portuguese vessels that of pilot; and the regulations of their marine confine him to the navigation of the ship, giving up to an inferior officer the duty of attending to the discharging or stowage of the hold when loading or unloading, and all other minutiæ of the affairs either at sea or in a harbor.

I was received on shore by all those persons with whom I had before had the pleasure of being acquainted, with the same friendliness which I always experienced at Pernambuco. Several English gentlemen offered me an apartment in their houses, until I obtained one of my own. I accepted the offer which was made to me by him through whose great kindness my health had been so much benefited after the severe attack of fever which I had suffered in the preceding year. The first few weeks were passed in visits to my friends and acquaintance, with some of whom I occasionally stayed a few days in the neighborhood of the town, which was now much deserted, according to the usual custom, at this season of the year.

I perceived a considerable difference in the appearance of Recife and of its inhabitants, although I had been absent from the place for so short a period. Several houses had been altered; the heavy somber latticework had given place, in many instances, to glass windows and iron balconies. Some few families had arrived here from Lisbon and three from England; the ladies of the former had shown the example of walking to mass in broad daylight; and those of the latter were in the habit of going out to walk toward the close of the day, for amusement. These improvements, being once introduced and practiced by a few persons, were soon adopted by some, who had been afraid to be the first, and by others who found that they were pleasant. Formal silks and satins, too, were becoming a less usual dress on high days and holidays, and were now much superseded by white and colored muslins, and other cotton manufactures. The men, likewise, who had in former times daily appeared in full dress suits of black, gold buckles, and cocked hats, had now, in many instances, exchanged these for nankeen pantaloons, half-boots, and round hats. Even the high and heavy saddle was now less in use, and that of more modern form was all the fashion. The sedan chairs, in which the ladies often go to church, and to pay visits to their friends, had now put on a much smarter appearance, and the men who carried them were dressed more dashingly. These cannot fail to attract the attention of strangers, in their gay clothes, their helmets and feathers, and their naked legs.

The country residences which had been lately built were also numerous; lands in the vicinity of Recife had risen in price; the trade of brick-making was becoming lucrative; work-people were in request; and besides many other spots of land, the tract between the villages of Poço da Panella and Monteiro, in extent about one mile, which in 1810 was covered with brushwood, had now been cleared; houses were building and gardens forming upon it. The great church of Corpo Santo, situated in that part of the town which is properly called Recife, was now finished, and various improvements were meditated. The time of advancement was come, and men, who had for many years gone on without making any change either in the interior or exterior of their houses, were now painting and glazing on the outside, and new furnishing within; modernizing themselves, their families, and their dwellings.

This spirit of alteration produced, in one case, rather ludicrous consequences. There was a lady of considerable dimensions, who had entered into this love of innovation, and carried it to a vast extent. She was almost equal in circumference and height, but notwithstanding this unfortunate circumstance, personal embellishments were not to be despised; she wished to dress in English fashion, and was herself decidedly of opinion that she had succeeded. Upon her head she wore a very small gypsy hat tied under the chin. Stays have only lately been introduced, but this improvement she had not yet adopted; still her gown was to be in English fashion too, and therefore was cut and slashed away, so as to leave most unmercifully in view several beauties which otherwise would have remained concealed. This gown was of muslin, and was worked down the middle and round the bottom in several colors; her shoes were as small as could be allowed; but the unfortunate redundance of size also reached the ankles and the feet, and thus rendering compression necessary; the superabundance which nature had lavishly bestowed projected and hung down over each side of the shoes.

I became acquainted and somewhat intimate with the *capitão-mor* of a neighboring district, from frequently meeting him in my evening visits to a Brazilian family. He was about to make the circuit of his district in the course of a few weeks, and invited one of my friends and myself to accompany him in this review or visit to his officers, to which we readily agreed.

The *capitães-móres*, captains-major, are officers of considerable power. They have civil as well as military duties to perform, and ought to be appointed from among the planters of most wealth and individual weight in the several *têrmos*, boundaries or districts; but the interest of family or of relations about the Court have occasioned deviations from this rule; and persons very unfit for these situations have been sometimes nominated to them.

The whole aspect of the government in Brazil is military. All men between the ages of sixteen and sixty must be enrolled either as soldiers of the line, as militia-men, or as belonging to the body of *Ordenanças*. Of the regular soldiers, I have already spoken in another place. Of the second class, each township has a regiment, of which the individuals, with the exception of the major and adjutant, and in some cases the colonel, do not receive any pay. But they are considered as embodied men, and as such are called out upon some few occasions, in the course of the year, to assemble in uniform, and otherwise ac-coutered. The expense which must be incurred in this re-spect of necessity precludes the possibility of many persons becoming members of this class, even if the government was desirous of increasing the number of militia regiments. The soldiers of these are subject to their captains, to the colonel, and to the governor of the province. The colonels are either rich planters, or the major or lieutenant-colonel of a regiment of the line is thus promoted to the command of one of these; in this case, and in this case only, he re-ceives pay. I am inclined to think that he ought to possess some property in the district, and that any deviation from this rule is an abuse; but I am not certain that the law so ordains. The majors and the adjutants are likewise oc-casionally promoted from the line; but whether they are regularly military men or planters, they receive pay, as their trouble in distributing orders, and in other arrange-ments connected with the regiment is considerable.

The third class, that of the *Ordenanças*, consisting of by far the largest portion of the white persons and of free mulatto men of all shades, have for their immediate chiefs the *capitães-móres*, who serve without pay, and all the persons who are connected with the *Ordenanças* are obliged likewise to afford their services gratuitously. Each district contains one *capitão-mor*, who is invariably a person possessing property in the part of the country to which he is appointed. He is assisted by a major, captains, and *alferes*, who are lieutenants or ensigns, and by sergeants and corporals. The duties of the *capitão-mor* are to see that every individual under his command has in his possession some species of arms; either a firelock, a sword, or a pike. He distributes the governor's orders through his district, and can oblige any of his men to take these orders to the nearest captain, who sends another peasant forward to the next captain, and so forth, all of which is done without any pay. A *capitão-mor* can also imprison for twenty-four hours, and send under arrest for trial a person who is accused of having committed any crime, to the civil magistrate of the town to which his district is immediately attached. Now, the abuses of this office of *capitão-mor* are very many, and the lower orders of free persons are much oppressed by these great men, and by their subalterns, down to the corporals. The peasants are often sent upon errands which have no relation to public business; for leagues and leagues these poor fellows are made to travel, for the purpose of carrying some private letter of the chief, of his captains, or of his lieutenants, without any remuneration. Indeed, many of these men in place seldom think of employing their slaves on these occasions, or of paying the free persons so employed. This I have witnessed times out of number; and have heard the peasants in all parts of the country complain: it is a most heavy grievance. Nothing so much vexes a peasant as the consciousness of losing his time and trouble in a service which is not required by his sovereign. Persons are sometimes confined in the stocks for days together, on some trifling plea, and are at last released with-

out being sent to the civil magistrate, or even admitted to
a hearing. However, I am happy to say that I am acquainted with some men whose conduct is widely different
from what I have above stated; but the power given to an
individual is too great, and the probability of being called
to an account for its abuse too remote, to insure the exercise
of it in a proper manner.

The free mulattos and free Negroes whose names are
upon the rolls, either of the militia regiments which are
commanded by white officers, or by those of their own
class and color, are not, properly speaking, subject to the
capitães-móres. These officers and the colonels of militia are
appointed by the supreme government, and the subaltern
officers are nominated by the governor of each province.

On the 28th January, 1812, the *capitão-mor* sent one
of his servants to summon us to his plantation, and to be
our guide. Early on the morning following, my friend, myself, our own two servants, and the boy who had been sent
to us by the *capitão-mor*, set forth on horseback in high
spirits; my friend and I expecting to see something new
and strange.

We proceeded to Olinda, and passed through its
wretchedly paved streets with much care. The country
which was to be seen in the distance was covered with
wood.

To those who are unaccustomed to a country that is
literally covered with woods, which prevent an extensive
view of the surrounding objects, and the free circulation of
air, the delightful sensations which are produced by a fine
green field, opening all at once to the sight, and swept by a
refreshing breeze, cannot possibly be felt. The plantation
of Paulistas is so situated. The buildings were numerous,
but most of them were low, and somewhat out of repair.
These are the dwelling house of the owner, which is spacious, and has one story above the ground floor; the chapel
with its large wooden cross erected upon the center of the
gable end; the mill, a square building without walls, its
roof being supported upon brick pillars; the long row of

Negro huts, the steward's residence, and several others of minor importance. These edifices are all of them scattered upon a large field, which is occupied by a considerable number of tame cattle; this is skirted by a dike which runs in front, but somewhat at a distance from the dwelling house of the owner, and through it runs the water which turns the mill. On the opposite side of the field is the chaplain's cottage, with its adjoining lesser row of Negro huts, its plantain garden, and its wide-spreading mango trees behind it. Beyond the principal house are low and extensive cane and meadow-lands, which are skirted on one side by the buildings of another small plantation, and bordered at a great distance by woods, which are situated upon the sides and summit of rising ground.

This valuable and beautiful plantation was in the possession of a near relation of our *capitão-mor*. We were acquainted with the son of the owner, who was chaplain to the estate, and had invited us to make his residence our resting place; this we did. He was prepared to receive us, and after having breakfasted, we proceeded to pay a visit to the old gentleman at the Great House, as the dwellings of the owners of plantations are called. He was unwell, and could not be seen; but we were received by his wife and two daughters. They made many inquiries about England, and conversed upon other subjects which they supposed we might be acquainted with. This estate was not much worked; the slaves led a most easy life, and the Great House was full of young children. Of these urchins several came in and out of the room; they were quite naked, and played with each other, and with some large dogs which were lying at full length upon the floor. These ebon cupids were plainly great favorites, and seemed to employ the greater part of the thoughts of the good ladies, the youngest of whom was on the wrong side of fifty; and even the priest laughed at their gambols. These excellent women and the good priest possess a considerable number of slaves, who are their exclusive property. It is their intention eventually to emancipate all of them, and that they may be prepared for the change, several of the men have been brought up as mechanics of different descriptions; and the women have been taught needlework, embroidery, and all branches of culinary knowledge. Thus, by the death of four individuals, who are now approaching to old age, will be set free about sixty persons, men, women, and children. As these people have been made acquainted with the intentions of their owners respecting them, it is not surprising that the behavior of many of them should be overbearing. To some, the deeds of manumission have been already passed conditionally, obliging them to serve as slaves until the death of the individual to whom they are subject. These papers cannot be revoked, and yet no ingratitude was feared; but among so considerable a number of persons, some instances of it cannot, I fear, fail to be experienced. The owners said that all their own immediate relations are rich, and not at all in need of assistance; and that therefore independent of other reasons connected generally with the system of slavery, these their children had no right to work for any one else. Of the slaves in question, only a few are Africans, the major part being mulattos and creole Negroes.

We returned to the cottage of the priest to dinner, and in the afternoon proceeded to the sugar plantation of Aguiar, belonging to the *capitão-mor*, which is distant from Paulistas five leagues, where we arrived about ten o'clock at night, much fatigued. Immediately beyond Paulistas is the narrow but rapid stream of Paratibe, which near to its mouth changes this name for that of Doce. We passed by four sugar mills this afternoon; that which bears the name of Utinga *de baixo* is situated in an amphitheater, being surrounded by high hills, covered with large trees. These woods have not been much disturbed, and therefore give refuge to enormous quantities of game, among which the *porco do mato*, or pig of the woods, is common. Many criminals and runaway Negroes are harbored in these woods. The inhabitants of Utinga seem to be shut out from all the rest of the world, as the path which leads from it is not immediately distinguished. The last three leagues, which we traversed in the dark, were covered with almost unbroken woods; the path through them is narrow, and the branches of the trees cross it in all directions; our guide rode in front, and many times did his head come in contact with them.

The dwelling of the *capitão-mor* is a large building of one story above the ground floor: the lower part of which forms the warehouse for the sugar and other articles which the estate produces. We ascended a wooden staircase, erected on the outside of the building, entered a small antechamber, and were received by our host and one of his sons, who conducted us into a spacious apartment beyond. A long table, and one of rather less dimensions, a couple of benches, and a few broken and unpainted chairs formed the whole furniture of these rooms. Four or five black boys, who were of a size too far advanced to wear the bow and arrow, but who were quite as little encumbered with dress as if they still might wield these dangerous weapons in the character of cupids, stood all astonishment to view the strange beings that had just arrived; and at all the doors were women's heads peeping to see whom we might be. The supper consisted as is usual of great quantities of meat, placed upon the table without arrangement.

At five o'clock in the morning, the *capitão-mor*, my friend, myself, and three servants proceeded to the distance of three leagues without any addition to our party; but we were soon joined by the adjutant of the district and several other officers, in uniforms of dark blue with yellow facings most monstrously broad—the gay cuffs reaching half way up to the elbows; they wore round hats with short feathers, straight swords of most prodigious length, and very loose nankeen pantaloons and boots; the former were thrust within the latter, which caused the higher part of the pantaloons to appear to be of preposterous width. We dismounted at a sugar plantation, being the third we had passed through this morning; here we were invited to stay to breakfast, but this we could not do, and were therefore regaled with pineapples and oranges. The owner of this place had taken great pains with his garden, and had reared several fruits which require much care; but it is strange that, although there are many which may be raised with very little trouble, still upon far the greater number of plantations even oranges are not to be found.

We arrived at midday at Santa Cruz, and had now reached the cotton country. The tract through which we had passed was for the most part well watered and well wooded, the marshy lands being less frequently interspersed than upon the journey of the preceding day. The sugar plantations were numerous; we saw eight of them this morning. The ground was often uneven, and we crossed one rather steep hill. The lands upon which we had now arrived, and those to which we were advancing, are altogether higher, and the grass upon them was now much burnt up, the "first waters" not having yet fallen. The soil in these parts retains less moisture than that of the country which we had left, and soon becomes too hard to be worked. The party was now much increased, and in the afternoon we proceeded to Pindoba, a cotton plantation of considerable extent; the owner of it is wealthy, and possesses many slaves. He received us in his dressing-gown, under which he wore a shirt, drawers and a pair of stockings. After the first greetings were over, he brought out a small bottle of liqueur made in the country, to which he himself helped his guests, one solitary glass, which was filled, and then emptied by each person, being made use of by the whole party. After supper a guitar player belonging to the house entertained us until a late hour, while our host sat upon a table smoking from a pipe of fully six feet in length. Several hammocks were slung in two large apartments, and each person either talked or went to sleep, or occasionally did one and the other, no form or ceremony being observed.

The peasants began to assemble early on the following morning, as three companies of the *Ordenanças* were to be reviewed. These were the first which were to undergo inspection, as the *capitão-mor* purposed visiting again the places through which we had passed on his return, and intended then to perform this duty. The men wore their usual dress of shirt and drawers, and perhaps a nankeen jacket and pantaloons were added, and most of them had muskets. The *capitão-mor* came forth this day in his scarlet uniform, and sat down near a table. The captain of the company which was about to be reviewed stood near him with the muster roll. The names of the privates were called over by the captain, and as each name was repeated by the sergeant, who stood at the doorway, the individual to whom it belonged came in and presented arms to the *capitão-mor*, then turned about and retired. It was truly ridiculous, but at the same time painful, to see the fright which the countenances of some of the poor fellows expressed, and their excessive awkwardness when they came to present themselves; while others displayed evident self-sufficiency; these were well-dressed, and performed every maneuver with as much neatness and promptitude as they were capable of, expressive of superior knowledge, and in hopes of admiration. There were of course many absentees, and for the nonappearance of these some reason was given by one of the officers of the company to which the man belonged, or by a neighbor. The excuses were usually received as all-sufficient, without any further inquiry being made. However the absence of one of the captains was not thus quietly acquiesced in, and therefore an officer was dispatched to his house to bring him to Pindoba under arrest. Whether this proceeded from some private pique, or from zeal for the public service, I do not pretend to determine, but he soon arrived in custody. He was put into one of the apartments of the house which we were inhabiting, and a sergeant was stationed at the door as a sentinel. The *capitão-mor* soon however relented, upon which he was released and allowed to return home.

At dinner the great man took the head of the table, and the owner of the house stood by and waited upon him. Everything was served up in enormous quantities, for the party was large, and this is the custom; there was no sort of regularity observed; every man helped himself to the dish which pleased him best, and this was oftentimes done with the knife which the person had been making use of upon his own plate, and by reaching across two or three of his neighbors for the purpose. A nice bit was not safe even upon one's own plate, being occasionally snatched up, and another less dainty given in return. Much wine was drunk during dinner, and the glasses were used in common. We soon rose from table, and the party, generally speaking, took the accustomed *sesta* or nap after dinner which is usual in warm climates. My friend and I walked out in the afternoon, but there was nothing to tempt us to go far, for the neighborhood possessed no natural beauty, and the dry weather had burnt up the grass, and had made the face of the country extremely dreary.

Early on the morrow about forty persons sallied forth for the village of Bom Jardim. It is distant from Pindoba one league and a half. We arrived there at seven o'clock. This village is built in the form of a square; the houses are low, but the church is large and handsome. Like the huts of Açu and of some other places, those of Bom Jardim are not whitewashed, and therefore the mud of which they are composed remains in its original color. The place contains about 500 inhabitants. We ascended a steep hill to arrive at it, and on the opposite side still another of equal heights is to be surmounted in proceeding farther inland. The village is situated upon a break of the hill. The soil is chiefly composed of red earth, approaching in places to a bright scarlet, with veins of yellow running through it; this is the description of soil, which is said to be the best adapted to the growth of cotton. Bom Jardim is a great rendezvous for the hawkers who are proceeding to the sertão, and for others who merely advance thus far. It is distant from Recife twenty good leagues, in a NE direction.

We discovered that mass was about to be said, and therefore we accompanied some of our party to the church. It was crowded; indeed it is a remark which I was fre-

quently led to make, that on Sundays and holidays, when
the peasantry assemble at the church doors, their numbers
must astonish those persons who merely pass through the
country without opportunities being afforded to them of
a more minute examination. The cottages upon the road
side do not promise so numerous a population as is on
these occasions to be seen; but from the thickness of the
woods and the lowness of the huts, even when a view of the
country is by any accident to be obtained from a high hill,
the dwellings of the lower orders of people are not to be
perceived; they are scattered all over the country; and
narrow paths which appear impassable or nearly so, and
are scarcely to be observed, often lead to four or five huts,
situated in the center of a wood or upon some low ground,
adapted to the cultivation of manioc and maize.

One company was reviewed at Bom Jardim, and
from hence a captain was deputed to continue the review
further into the country. We rode this afternoon one
league to the house of Captain Anselmo, being so far upon
our return. On our way to this place we saw the woods on
one side of the road on fire.

Captain Anselmo resides upon a cotton plantation
which is his own property, and is cultivated by about forty
Negroes. The house is situated upon the shelf of a steep
hill, with a beautiful plain below, upon which trees are
thickly scattered. At the foot of the hill is a large fish-pond,
through which a rivulet runs in the rainy season. The
owner has lately enclosed a piece of land, and was making
a garden upon the borders of the pond. The dwelling house
was new and had a second floor; it was very clean and well
furnished. This was the most pleasantly situated and the
best arranged mansion which we visited during this journey; the huts for the slaves were well built and looked comfortable. Here we were entertained with such music as has
as yet found its way into these parts of the country. Three
Negroes with bagpipes attempted to play a few tunes
while we were at dinner, but they seemed to play in different keys from each other, and sometimes each appeared to

have struck up a tune of his own composing. I think I never heard so bad an attempt at producing harmonious sounds as the *charameleiros* made. The possession of a band of these bespeaks a certain degree of superiority, consequently the planters pride themselves upon their musicians.

Our party could not let pass this opportunity of being together without practicing the amusement of the *entrudo*, although the usual time of its celebration was yet distant one week. On the day subsequent to that of our arrival, dinner was scarcely over before the *farinha*, the bananas, the rice, and other dainties upon the table were hurled at each other's heads; soon the smart uniform coats were taken off, and in his shirt-sleeves each man began this civil war with heart and soul. Everything was borne with perfect good humor, and at last, fatigued and bedaubed, all of us retired to the hammocks which had been provided for the party. But as our evil stars would have it, a brave captain closed quietly all the shutters (as the moon was shining very bright into the room), and then he placed himself near to an enormous jar of water, which stood in one corner of the apartment, and with a small pitcher in his hand soon dealt around him its contents, awakening us with repeated showers, and obliging us to take shelter under the chairs and tables. This, and other jokes allied to it, continued until the break of day, when we prepared for a continuation of our journey. One company was reviewed here.

We proceeded to the house of Captain Paulo Travasso, distant one league. At this place the *entrudo* was continued more violently than before; for even the blackened pots and pans from the kitchen were introduced to besmear each other's faces. We obtained here a view of the females belonging to the house; but everywhere else they had been too rigorously guarded, or were naturally too reserved to enable us to see them. Some excuse was made by the young men who were acquainted with the family, to draw them into the sport; and the ladies and their slaves were nothing loath to see and to participate in what was going forward. A circumstance occurred which created much laughter, and which is but too characteristic. One man whom we met at this place had all along begged of those who were engaged in the sport that they would not wet him, because he was unwell; however it was seen that he did not observe toward others that forbearance which he entreated from them toward himself. One of our party seeing this attacked him with a large silver ladle filled with water; the man ran out of the house, and the other followed; but when they were at some distance from it, he turned upon his pursuer, and drawing his knife, stood at some distance, threatening to stab him if he advanced. The other, striking his left side at the place in which knives are usually carried, likewise threatened him, and without delay advanced toward him, having picked up a thick stick as he approached. But his adversary did not like the thoughts of a close combat, and soon set off at full speed, with his knife in his hand. In this manner he entered the back door of the house, while he of the silver ladle took the front door. They met in the apartment from which they had started, when the latter opened his waistcoat, and showed that he had not a knife; thus proving before the whole party, that he of the knife had run away from one who was unarmed. This was quite sufficient; the women made a general attack upon him: he went to the stable, mounted his horse, and set forth; but his misfortunes had not yet ended, for the path by which he must retreat lay under two of the windows of the house, and as he passed, two large tubs of water drenched him and his steed, which immediately quickened its pace, amidst the hooting of everyone present.

We continued our journey in the afternoon to a sugar plantation, the property of Captain João Soares, where we remained until the following day. Some of us were tired of the *entrudo*, and therefore sought shelter in the mill and adjoining out-houses, when we saw the sport again commencing; but we were about to be attacked, when we gained the rooms of one of the buildings, and from hence could not be dislodged.

I had frequently seen the *saboeiro* or soap-tree, which

is to be chiefly found in these districts. It is a large shrub,
which puts forth numerous branches in every direction,
so that when it is in full leaf, it has somewhat the appearance of trees that have been clipped, (as was formerly
practiced in gardens,) which is increased by the leaves
being small and growing very close to each other. The re-
ceptacle of the seed is about the size of a small plum; when
this is put into water, and rubbed with some violence, it
produces the same effect as that which is caused by soap
in water, and it has the same property of cleansing. The
pão do alho or garlic tree, is to be met with in great abundance in these districts. The name is derived from the simil-
itude of the smell of the leaves and the wood of this plant
to garlic. The tree abounds so greatly, and, I suppose, reminded the first settlers so much of one of their favorite
European culinary ingredients that it has given name to a
town, and to a whole district.

About five o'clock in the afternoon we proceeded to
Limoeiro, a large and thriving village. It is composed of
one street of about three-quarters of a mile in length,
which is closed at one end by the church and vicarage:
this building belonged formerly to the Jesuits. The trade of
Limoeiro with the interior is considerable, and particularly on the day of the market, which is held weekly, the
bustle is excessive. These days seldom pass without some
murders being committed, or at least many wounds and
blows being given; but the markets of Nazareth or Lagoa
d'Anta are those which are particularly famed for the disturbances that usually take place there. These became so
considerable at one time, that the governor found it necessary to issue orders for a patrol to keep the peace on market
days.

The *capitão-mor* had still several posts to visit, which
would delay him for a considerable time; therefore as my
friend was anxious to return to Recife, we left our party,
with much regret. We proceeded to Recife on the evening
of the 6th February.

I heard one of the sugar planters bitterly complaining of his poverty, and that his want of hands to work his mill obliged him to give up the cultivation of much of the best land of his estate. Soon after he had uttered these complaints, the conversation turned upon saddle-horses and their trappings; and he then told us that he had lately purchased a new saddle and bridle, which he wished us to see. These new trappings were most superb affairs; the saddle was made of morocco leather and green velvet, and silver-headed nails and plates of the same metal were profusely scattered and placed upon all parts of this and of the bridle. He told us that the whole had cost him four hundred *mil reis*, about 110*l*. This sum of money would have purchased four slaves. But the matter did not end here, for he opened a drawer in which were strewed several broken silver-spoons, spurs, etc. and he said that he was collecting a sufficient quantity of this metal for the purpose of having his groom's horse ornamented in the same manner as his own.

The free persons of color who inhabit the tract of country through which we passed are more numerous than I had previously imagined. The companies of Ordenanças vary much in strength; some consist of one hundred and fifty men and more, and others of not above fifty. The peasantry of the *mata*, that is, of the country which lies between the plentiful well-watered districts of the coast and the sertões, have not a general good character. The miserable life which they, oftener than others, are obliged to lead from the want of water and of provisions, seems to have an unfavorable effect upon them; they are represented as being more vindictive and more quarrelsome, and less hospitable than their neighbors. To say that a man is a *matuto da mata*, a woodman of the wood, is no recommendation to him.

IX

OF PLANTERS AND
FESTIVALS

After the journey to Bom Jardim, I did not again leave Recife for any length of time until I entered with a friend into a scheme of farming. It had been greatly my wish to remove from the town into the country, from preference, rather than from any other cause.

In the beginning of April, 1812, we entered the sugar plantation of Jaguaribe, distant from Recife four leagues, in a northward direction, and about one league from the coast; it had upon it several slaves, oxen, machinery, and implements, which enabled the new tenant to enter it immediately.

About the middle of May I removed to Jaguaribe. The road to it is through the plantation of Paulistas, from whence, after crossing the Paratibe, a narrow path leads to the left through a deep wood for nearly one league. A steep hill is to be surmounted, and its corresponding declivity carefully descended. The wood continues to a break in the hill, on the side nearest to Jaguaribe. On reaching this spot there was a view before me which would in most situations be accounted very beautiful, but in this delightful country so many fine prospects are continually presenting themselves that I opened upon this with few feelings of pleasure at the sight. I cannot avoid owning that the advantages of the place as a plantation occupied my mind more deeply than its beauties. Immediately before me was a cottage and a row of Negro huts, surrounded by banana trees, standing upon a shelf of the hill. Beyond these to the left was the narrow, but far extending valley, upon whose nearest border were situated the buildings of Jaguaribe upon an open field, with the hills behind, and in front was the rivulet. To the right was a deep dell, with an expanse of country not thickly covered with wood; and rather in advance, but also to the right, were numerous deep-colored mangroves, which pointed out that a stream of considerable size ran down among them. On the other side of the nearest of these mangroves, and yet not very far, was the high peak of São Bento, with the manioc, and maize lands, and wood upon its side, and the path winding up through them, which is at times concealed, and at times in view; but the buildings are not to be seen, though the tolling of the chapel bell may be often heard, from the spot upon which I was standing.

I was under the necessity of taking up my abode in the vestry of the chapel, as the Great House was still occupied. The Negroes were already at work for us, and under the direction of a proper *feitor* or manager. The whole neighborhood was astonished at the place I had determined to inhabit, until some other dwelling presented itself. I was certainly not comfortably situated, for the vestry consisted of only one apartment, with a doorway to the field and another into the church, the latter being without a door; the church was unfinished, and was the resort of bats and owls; however, it was principally my unconcern respecting ghosts which my neighbors were surprised at. A Negro boy and myself remained at night to encounter these, if any should appear, and to receive our constant visitors the bats. My companion rolled himself up upon the ground in a piece of baize and a mat, and thus cased, was quite safe. I slept in a hammock, and oftentimes these unwelcome guests alighted upon it, as if they had come for the chance of a toe or a finger making its appearance, upon which they might fix. This way of living did not last long, nor did I wish that it should.

The house of which I have spoken as being situated upon a shelf of the hill, and as looking down upon the valley, was soon without an inhabitant, and therefore to this I removed. It was large, but the floors of the rooms were without bricks, and the interior walls had not been whitewashed for ages, and some of them had never undergone the operation. I received visits and presents, as is customary, from my immediate neighbors—the white persons, and those of color who aspire to gentility; and indeed many individuals of the lower class did not neglect to come and offer their services to the newcomer, whose character and disposition toward them they judged that it was necessary to become acquainted with. In many instances the wives of the latter description of visitors came also, and brought sweetmeats, fruit or flowers. I received them all, sitting in my hammock; the men sat round on chairs, but the women generally squatted down upon the floor, though it was formed of earth. I talked to them of my intentions, and of my wish to conciliate, and I heard much of bickerings and squabbles among those of their own rank, and of feuds between their superiors, the same stories being related to me in many different ways. They were much surprised that I should wear so much clothes, saying, that I ought to do as they did, and be unencumbered; and their advice I soon followed. I was much amused, and for some days these visits took up the largest portion of my time.

The lands around me, to the north, belonged to the Benedictine friars; and to the east to an old lady; those of the latter were much neglected, but those which were possessed by the former were in high order. To the south, beyond the wood through which I passed in coming to Jaguaribe, are the lands of Paulistas; and to the west and northwest are some excellent cane lands, belonging to a religious lay brotherhood of free Negroes of Olinda, which were tenanted by and subdivided among a great number of persons of low rank, whites, mulattos, and blacks.

The work went on regularly, and I had soon very little in which to employ my time, excepting in those things by which I might think proper to amuse myself.

In the beginning of June, it was necessary that I should visit Goiana; however I took a circuitous route for the purpose of seeing something new. I was accompanied by an old free man of color and by Manoel, a faithful African. We slept the first night at Aguiar, the estate of the *capitão-mor* with whom I had travelled to Bom Jardim; and on the following morning proceeded through several sugar plantations. We rested at midday at Purgatorio, a small cotton and manioc plantation, but we could not purchase anything of which to make a dinner, and therefore, as was usual on such occasions, we smoked in place of eating. When the sun had declined a little, we again set forth. A few of the sugar plantations through which we passed in the afternoon were in a decayed state. We stopped at a cottage, and begged the owner to sell us a fowl, but she refused;—we had not eaten anything this day. I was loath so to do, but I could not avoid saying that she *must* sell one, that I did not mind the price, but that hunger would not allow me to let her do as she pleased in this case. She fixed upon one, and made me pay exorbitantly for it. We parted in the end very good friends; she offered me some herbs with which to cook the bird, and after this reconciliation we again advanced.

I stayed only two days at Goiana, for I soon accomplished the object of my journey, which was to obtain twenty Indian laborers from Alhandra. My return to Jaguaribe was by the usual road.

The day after my arrival at my new home, I rode to Recife, and had on the following day an attack of ague. I had exposed myself lately too much to the sun, and had been several times wet through. The disorder left me in a fortnight; and I set off for Jaguaribe; but midway I was drenched with rain, and reaching that place much tired, went to sleep unintentionally in my hammock, without changing my clothes. In the morning I felt that the ague was returning, and therefore ordered my horse and rode out to try to shake off the attack, which the peasants say it is possible to do. However, while I was talking with a neighbor, on horseback at his door, the ague came on, and I was unable to return to my own dwelling.

The next day the Indians from Alhandra arrived; they had imbibed strange notions of the riches of an Englishman; and their captain told me that they knew I was

very rich and could afford to give higher wages than anyone else. I tried to undeceive them in this respect, but all
to no purpose. I offered the usual rate of labor in the country; but their characteristic obstinacy had entered into
them, and they preferred returning as they came to any
abatement of their first demand, although this was 25 per
cent higher than any person had ever been known to give
for daily labor. They dined, placed their wallets upon their
shoulders, and went their way. One of my people said, as
they disappeared, ascending the hill, beyond the field,
"They had rather work for anyone else for half the money,
than lower their demands to you."

I was removed from this neighbor's house, after a few
days, in a hammock; but finding that the disorder increased, I sent for the manager, an old man of color, whose
wife attended upon me. By my desire, he collected a sufficient number of bearers, as it was my wish to be carried
to Recife. About five o'clock in the afternoon we set off;
there were sixteen men to bear the hammock by turns, and
the manager was likewise in company; of these persons
only two were slaves. After we had passed the wood, and
had arrived upon a good road, the bearers proceeded at a
long walk approaching to a run. Their wild chorus, which
they sung as they went along—their mischief in throwing
stones at the dogs by the road side, and in abuse, half-
joking, half-wishing for an opportunity of quarrelling,
confident in their numbers, and that as they were in the
service of a white man he would bring them out of any
scrape—was very strange, and had I been less unwell, this
journey would have much amused me. As we passed
through Olinda, a woman asked my men if they carried a
dead body (for it is in this manner that they are brought
from a distance for interment). One of the bearers answered, "No, it is the devil"; and then turning to me, said,
"Is it not so, my master?" I said, "Yes," and the good
woman walked away, saying, "Ave Maria, the Lord for-
bid." The wind was high and some rain fell as we crossed
the Olinda sands; we arrived at Recife between nine and

ten o'clock. The bearers stopped before we approached the gateway at the entrance of the town, that each man might, in some way or other, conceal his long, unlawful knife; without one of these weapons no peasant or great man leaves his home, notwithstanding the prohibition.

I became gradually worse, until my recovery was not expected; but the kind, attentive hand of another Englishman here again was stretched forth. My former friend had left the country, but another supplied his place, and from him I received every brotherly kindness.

As soon as I was well enough to remove, I took a small cottage at the village of Monteiro, that I might have the advantage of better air than that of Recife, and yet not be too far distant from medical advice. Here I passed my time very pleasantly in daily intercourse with a most worthy Irish family, of whom I shall always preserve recollections of gratitude for the kindness which I received at that time and on other occasions. On the night of my arrival at Monteiro, one of my pack horses was stolen, but the animal was recognized some weeks afterwards by a boy who was in my service; the man into whose hands he had fallen happened to pass through the village, and thus I recovered the horse. It is astonishing to what a great extent horse stealing has been carried in a country which abounds so much with these animals. It is almost the only species of robbery, for the practicing of which regular gangs of men have been formed; but these fellows will sometimes also chance to lay hold of a stray ox or cow.

I was most anxious to return to Jaguaribe, and about the middle of October was making preparations for the purpose when the manager arrived from the plantation with the intelligence that one of his assistants had been attacked two nights before, and nearly killed, by some persons who had been commissioned to perform this deed in revenge of some real or imagined injury which the man had committed. This determined my proceedings; the following morning I set off with the manager and a servant, to see the wounded man.

Much time had been lost, and the cane ought to have been planted for the crop of the following year; the Negroes in my possession could not perform what ought to be done in proper time, and therefore I collected free laborers for the purpose; and in a short period between thirty and forty men, some of whom brought their families, moved on to the lands of the plantation; and most of them erected hovels of palm leaves, in which they dwelt; but a few of them were accommodated with huts of mud. There were Indians, mulattos, free Negroes, and slaves working together—a motley crew.

I had now taken up my abode at the house which was usually inhabited by the owner or tenant; this was a low, but long mud cottage, covered with tiles, and white-washed within and without; it had bricked floors, but no ceiling. There were two apartments of tolerable dimensions, several small rooms, and a kitchen. The chief entrance was from a sort of square, formed by the several buildings belonging to the estate. In front was the chapel; to the left was a large dwelling house unfinished, and the Negro huts, a long row of small habitations, having much the appearance of almshouses, without the neatness of places of this description in England; to the right was the mill worked by water, and the warehouse or barn in which the sugar undergoes the process of claying; and to the view of these buildings may be added the pens for the cattle, the carts, heaps of timber, and a small pond through which the water runs to the mill. At the back of the house was the large open field, the milldam beyond, and cottages, manioc lands and trees along the valley, bordered on each side by steep hills covered with thick woods.

Oftentimes I have sat at night upon the threshhold of the door, after all my people had retired to their habitations; they have supposed that I was asleep; then I have heard the whisperings in the Negro huts, and have observed some one leave his house, and steal away to visit an acquaintance, residing at some distance; or there has been some feast or merrymaking. Neighboring Negroes have been invited, and have crept in during the evening unperceived. It is on these occasions that plans for deceiving the master are contrived. Then the slave-owner who is aware of such secret practices, and reflects, must feel how little avail all his regulations, all his good management.

At other times far different ideas from these have occupied my mind; I have thought of the strange life I was leading; a remembrance of feudal times in Europe has crossed me, and I could not forbear comparing with them the present state of the interior of Brazil. The great power of the planter, not only over his slaves, but his authority over the free persons of lower rank; the respect which is required by these barons from the free inhabitants of their lands; the assistance which they expect from their tenants in case of insult from a neighboring equal; the dependence of the peasants, and their wish to be under the peculiar protection of a person of wealth who is capable of relieving them from any oppression, and of speaking in their behalf to the governor, or to the chief judge; all these circumstances combined tend to render the similarity very great. I even felt the power which had unintentionally fallen into my hands. I had collected a considerable number of free workmen, and the estate was respected for miles round. Many of these fellows would have committed almost any crime under the impression that my protection would screen them.

While I was unwell at Recife and Monteiro, the manager and his wife had taken possession of the house; and here they remained for some time after my return. Thus, I lived literally among these people; I had indeed my meals alone, but generally two or three of the persons employed upon the plantation were in the room, while I breakfasted or dined, and they stood or sat talking to me. Anyone reached me a plate or aught else for which I asked, if he happened to be near to what I wanted.

I had become somewhat intimate in several families of the neighborhood; but was the most amused with my acquaintance in those of secondary rank, where there is less ceremony than among persons of the first class. In the former, the females often appear when the visitor is a neighbor, has concerns with the master of the house, and becomes intimate with him.

The Festival of São Bento was to be celebrated about the close of the year in the adjoining plantation, belonging to the monks of whom he is the patron saint. The convent is at Olinda, and there the abbot resides; the fraternity is rich, possessing much landed property. Upon the estate adjoining to Jaguaribe, manioc, maize, rice, and other articles of food are cultivated, with which the convent is supplied. The slaves upon it are in number about one hundred, of all ages; and the last African died while I resided in that part of the country. The festival, at which I intended to be present, was to our Lady of the Rosary, the patroness of Negroes. The expense which was to be incurred was subscribed for by the slaves of the estate, and the festival was entirely managed by them. Three friars attended to officiate at the altar; but the lights, the fireworks, and all other necessary articles were provided for by a committee of the slaves. The manager of the estate was a mulatto slave who made me a visit upon my arrival at Jaguaribe, and on the occasion of the festival came to invite me to the *novena* and to the *festa* (the nine previous evenings and the festival); or rather he came to request that I would not fail to go, as he feared that my people and his might quarrel. I went with a large party of men and women; we ascended the hill, and on our arrival at its summit, I was invited by one of the black women to enter her cottage, the same invitation being made to several other persons of our party. The chapel is placed quite upon the highest point of the hill; and the house in which the friars dwell, when they come to the estate, and the row of Negro huts, form a semicircle about it, thus in part enclosing the chapel. These habitations look down upon the broad river of Maria Farinha, winding below among the mangroves, and there are several creeks on the opposite side, which look like so many branches.

The crowd which had assembled was considerable, and was not a little increased by my free workmen, some of whom were unmarried men, unencumbered, and ready for any mischief. I was armed with a long pike and the large knife of the country; and had brought three of my slaves, accoutered much in the same manner—three resolute Africans upon whom I could depend, and whose business it was closely to watch their master. Before the commencement of the prayers and singing in the chapel, the black people extended several mats upon the ground in the open air; and our party sat down upon them to converse and to eat cakes and sweatmeats, of which many kinds were exposed for sale in great abundance. All went on quietly for three nights, for the mulatto manager forbade the sale of rum; but on the fourth night some liquor unfortunately found its way up the hill, and Nicolau, the manager, came in haste to inform me that a few of my Indians were earnestly bent on quarrelling with a party of his people. I rose from the mat upon which I had been seated, and followed by my body guard, accompanied him back to the spot, where I soon saw that a fight had commenced; persuasion was of no avail, and therefore my Negroes made use of the butt-ends of their pikes, and brought an Indian to the ground, who was delivered over to Simam, one of my fellows; and I desired the two slaves who remained to assist the São Bento Negroes. I thus proved that I would not uphold my own people if they acted irregularly; and the matter fortunately ended with only some trifling bruises, and one broken head. The Indian was conveyed home by Simam, who returned to tell me that he had placed the man in the stocks, with the intent of sobering him. No more quarrels were entered into; for this affair quite sickened all those who might have been so inclined. In the morning the Indian was set at liberty, and he quietly went off to his work, not being much the worse.

I had great pleasure in witnessing the most excellent arrangements of this plantation; the Negroes are as happy as persons in a state of slavery can be; but although the tasks are, comparatively speaking, easy, and corporal punishments are only resorted to for children, still the great object at which they aim is to be free, and to purchase the freedom of their children. One man, who was a fisherman by trade, had obtained the manumission of his wife, though he was still a slave himself, with the intent that if she should still have any more children, they might be free; and he purposed afterwards purchasing his own freedom, and that of his young ones. Several instances of the same behavior are frequently occurring upon the estates belonging to these and other friars. Thus everyone wishes to be a free agent; and it is this feeling alone which makes a São Bento Negro do all in his power to be able to act for himself; for very probably he may be obliged to labor with more diligence to obtain his living as a free man than as a slave. The emancipated Negro oftentimes becomes an excellent member of society, for he contracts habits of industry in which he continues; but again, if he has been hardly treated by a rigorous master, he becomes disgusted with, and indifferent to life, is rendered callous to shame, and drags on an idle, miserable existence.

Another festival was to take place at one of the chapels upon the coast, which is dedicated to our Lady of the Conception. This was distant one league and a half from Jaguaribe; however, we formed a party and mounted our horses one moonlight evening; the females riding behind their husbands and relations, with a sheet or counterpane thrown over the horse's haunches, upon which they sat. We came out upon the seashore at the church of our Lady of the O. (of which I shall presently speak,) not far from the Fort of Pão Amarelo, and from thence proceeded along the sands to the place of our destination. I was introduced to the family of an old Portuguese who resided here: his son had just taken orders as a secular priest, and was to say his first mass on the day of the festival. There were puppet shows, tumblers, and all their attendants in great abundance; fireworks and bonfires, noise, bustle, and no lack of quarrelling. Within the chapel there was a display of wax tapers, praying, singing, and music, as is usual.

As soon as the church service was ended we mounted our horses, and rode back to Our Lady of the O. We alighted at a cottage which stood near to the church, the inhabitants of which were acquainted with some of our party; the moon was bright and the breeze moderate. We sat down upon mats before the door, and were regaled with quantities of young coconuts, a most delightful fruit when they are in this state. Some of us walked down toward the beach; the tide was out, and I observed several large blocks of hewn stone, partly buried in the sand, below high watermark. I inquired what had caused them to be there, and was answered, that a church had formerly stood upon that spot; and I heard then, and afterwards often saw, that the sea was making considerable encroachments along the coast, to the distance of half a league or more each way. The new church of Our Lady of the O. was now building, at the distance of about three hundred yards from the shore.

The fame of this most powerful lady has reached far and wide, and from the interior to the distance of 150 leagues persons who were afflicted with disorders which had been considered incurable by human means have come down to make their offerings to this avaricious personage, whose powerful intercession is not to be obtained unless she is in return well paid for her trouble.

As the road from the sertão to the seashore was by Jaguaribe, I saw many of the travellers; I conversed with many wealthy persons, whose sole errand was to offer part of their possessions, upon condition of relief from the malady under which they suffered.

The miracles of Our Lady of the O. are performed in three ways—by prayer from the patient—by drinking the water of the spring, or by application of some of it to the part affected—and by eating, or outwardly applying, a small quantity of the salt which oozes from the wall against which the High Altar stands.

The mill was continually at work; I usually took the first watch, and superintended the business until midnight; several of my neighbors and their families came to amuse themselves in conversation, and others came for the purpose of eating sugar cane, of which every one who has tasted must be fond.

About this time a female slave died in childbed who was generally regretted. She was a good servant, and an excellent wife and mother. The grief of her husband bore much the appearance of insanity; he would not eat until the following day, and then he only tasted food from the persuasion of one of his children. Until the time of my departure from Pernambuco, he had not recovered his former spirits, and he never spoke of his wife without tears in his eyes. Even some of the other slaves were, for a few days after her death, unsettled; the rude instruments upon which they were in the habit of playing in the evening at their doors, were laid aside—all merriment was discontinued for some time.

I was requested about this period to be bride's man at the marriage of a mulatto couple. I agreed, and on the day appointed, set forth for Paratibe, accompanied by a free servant and a slave on horseback. I arrived about ten o'clock, and found a large party of people of color assembled; the priest soon arrived, and he too was of the same caste. Breakfast of meat and *pirão* (a paste made of *farinha*) was placed upon the table; some part of the company sat down and ate, others stood, doing the same, and others again, as if they were afraid of losing a minute's conversation, continued to talk loudly, and without ceasing. I have witnessed few such scenes of confusion. At last we proceeded to the church, to which I begged to be permitted to ride, for the distance was considerable, and I was somewhat lame from an accident; as soon as the ceremony was over, we returned to the house. The bride was of a dark brown color, for her father was a Negro, and her mother of mixed blood; she was dressed in a rose-colored silk gown, and a black veil was thrown over her head and shoulders; she wore white shoes and white stockings with open clocks. The bridegroom was also of dark color; he wore a coat of brown cloth, a waistcoat of brocaded silk and nankeen pantaloons; he had on shoes with large buckles and a cocked hat. Both of these persons were young, and they seemed to be dreadfully hampered with the increased stock of apparel which they carried. The scene at dinner was a counterpart of the breakfast affair, with the addition of more noise and more confusion, which were caused by a larger assemblage of people, and more plentiful draughts of wine and rum. I escaped as soon as possible; but would not on any account have missed being present at this day's work.

On the night of Christmas eve, I did not go to bed; for we were to hear the *Missa do Galo*, or cock mass, as is customary. The priest arrived, and the night was spent merrily. This person did not at that time come regularly as a chaplain, but he was so engaged afterwards.

X

PLANTATION LIFE
AT JAGUARIBE

About the middle of January, 1813, I went to stay for some
days at the cottage of an acquaintance, who resided upon
the plain of Barbalho, for the purpose of purchasing a few
horses. This place is near to the village of Monteiro; but
it is on the opposite side of the river. Barbalho is a plain
of some extent, upon which cattle are turned out to feed;
the soil of it is a stiff dark-colored clay, and the grass which
grows upon it is of a coarse species; this becomes quite dry
during the summer months, and when in this state it is set
on fire, that the tender shoots which again spring up may
serve as food for the animals that are to graze upon it. The
fire will run along the ground, urged by a fresh breeze; it
will sometimes contract, and at others spread each way,
presenting to the beholders a fiery wall. The sight is grand;
it is upon a large scale, which gives to it a terrific appearance. The inhabitants of the skirts of this plain carefully
preserve a circle around their houses and gardens, clear of
vegetation, apprehensive of some inconsiderate traveller
who may chance to light his pipe as he goes along, and
throw away unextinguished the fire stick of which he has
made use.

The person with whom I was staying persuaded me
to ride with him to the sugar plantation of Uninha, which
is distant six leagues to the southward of Barbalho; he
described the place as being very beautiful, and I con-
sented. The sugar plantation of Camasari, belonging to
the Carmelite friars, is in high order, that is, the slaves and
cattle are in good condition, and everything upon it appeared cheerful; but it does not yield so much produce as
it might, if the strength of the laborers were pushed to the
utmost. I looked into the mill, which is turned by water,
and saw some handsome mulatto girls feeding the mill

with cane; they were dressed in petticoats of printed cotton, and smocks of cambric muslin, and they wore upon their necks and in their ears gold ornaments; they were singing in parts very tolerably. The difference between the plantations which belong to convents, and those which are possessed by individuals who reside upon them, and have a direct interest in every trifling increase or decrease of the gains, is very striking.

At length we arrived at the plantation of Uninha, which is situated upon an extensive field, composed of uneven ground; and watered by several springs. The mill is turned by oxen, which is a late improvement, horses being usually employed where water cannot be obtained. We dined with the owner, and he returned with us to Barbalho in the afternoon. I was much delighted with the day's amusement. This was the most beautiful part of the country which I visited, taken as a whole. The hills and the valleys are not high or extensive, but they are decidedly marked. Here cultivation formed a considerable feature in the country, the cane lands were extensive, and the mills for its manufacture into sugar numerous.

On my return from Uninha, I wished still to remain at Barbalho for a few days, and therefore the owner of the cottage at which I was staying went on to Jaguaribe, to remain there until I could join him. I stayed with Manoel and Simam. One morning Manoel had gone to cut a bundle of grass, and on his return met with an old acquaintance, a creole Negro; they quarrelled by the way, and as they came near to where I was residing, the matter became serious, and blows were given and received, both of the men being armed with long poles. Simam saw this, took up a drawn sword which was lying upon a chair, and ran out to assist his comrade. I went out to put a stop to the business, and discovered that Simam had cut an enormous gash in the fellow's head; the man was brought into the cottage, and his wound was dressed. An acquaintance of mine happened now to come in, and he took charge of the Negro, and carried him home to his master. The Negro

was taking a load of grass for the governor's horses, who
was residing at Monteiro, which is within half a mile.
Notice would have been taken of the affair immediately,
owing to the circumstance of the Negro being employed
for the governor, if His Excellency had not been informed
that the offending Negroes (for such I consider mine to
have been) belonged to an Englishman, upon which no
more inquiry was made; and as it was discovered that the
master had nothing to do with the affray, no cognizance
was taken of the matter by the military power. If the owner
of the wounded slave had chosen so to do, he might have
put me to much expense and trouble, for he might have
accused my Negroes of assaulting his; but the law of itself
seldom does anything. Even in cases of murder the prose-
cutor, or accuser as he is called, has it at his option to bring
the trial forward or not; if he can be bribed or otherwise
persuaded to give up the accusation, the matter drops to
the ground. Thus the spirit of law is changed, from the
principle of bringing an offender to justice for the general
good of society to that of prosecuting in revenge for the
crime which he has committed against an individual.

Soon after my return to Jaguaribe, I was one evening
surprised at the arrival of a white man in uniform of blue
and red, and accompanied by a great number of loaded
horses, and of men, who were dressed in leather after the
manner of the sertão. He delivered to me a letter, which I
discovered not to be for me, but for an Englishman who
was occasionally with me; however, I of course requested
him to stay, and gave directions for the accommodation
of his followers. He was a commandant from the interior,
distant 130 leagues, in the back settlements of the province
of Paraíba, at the foot of the Serra do Teixeira. He had
put on board of *jangadas* at Paraíba a considerable quantity of cotton, which he had brought down from his estate,
and he was now travelling to Recife for the purpose of receiving it, and of purchasing necessaries or rather luxuries
for his family, to which he appeared to be extremely attached. We soon became intimate, and when he proceeded

to Recife at the close of a few days, he left some of his men and horses at Jaguaribe. It is among the inhabitants of places so remote as the district from which he came, that clanship more particularly exists. He had with him ten persons, most of whom were his *compadres*, that is, the commandant was sponsor to one of the children of each. This relationship is accounted very sacred in Brazil, and I believe in all Roman Catholic countries; it is a bond of brotherhood, which permits the poor man to speak to his superior with a kind of endearing familiarity, and unites them in links of union, of which the nonobservance would be sacrilegious. The commandant made me several visits from Recife, and after a delay of two months, he set off on his return homeward.

The Indians who were in my service occasionally requested leave to dance in front of my dwelling; I usually complied, and was often much amused. A large fire was made, that we might the better see what was going on; and that the evening might be rendered more entertaining, I frequently invited some of my neighbors. The dance commenced by two men stepping forward, and walking round and round, taking a circuit of a few yards, one of them singing, or rather reciting in a low voice some ditty of his own language, and the other playing upon a shrill pipe. As they went on, at intervals they gave a hop or a skip; soon, a woman joined them, and walked after them, and then another man came forward, and so forth, until a large ring was formed and the pace was quickened. It was always expected that some liquor should be prepared for them, and each of these persons, as they felt inclined to take any of it, stepped out of the ring, and returned again as soon as they had drunk. They continued dancing as long as any rum was produced, the women as well as the men relishing this, their means of inspiration; for as the quantities were increased, some new song was introduced, the tones became louder, and their articulation more rapid.

The free people of color, too, would sometimes dance;

but they only asked permission of me, and held their merrymaking at the door of one of their own huts. Their dances were like those of the African Negroes. A ring was formed; the guitar player sat down in a corner, and began a simple tune, which was accompanied by some favorite song, of which the burthen was often repeated, and frequently some of the verses were extempore, and contained indecent allusions. One man stepped out into the center of the ring, and danced for some minutes, making use of lascivious attitudes, until he singled out a woman, who then came forward, and took her turn in movements not less indecent, and thus the amusement continued sometimes until daybreak. The slaves would also request to be permitted to dance; their musical instruments are extremely rude. One of them is a sort of drum, which is formed of a sheep skin, stretched over a piece of the hollowed trunk of a tree; and another is a large bow with one string, having half of a coconut shell or of a small gourd strung upon it. This is placed against the abdomen, and the string is struck with the finger, or with a small bit of wood. When two holidays followed each other uninterruptedly, the slaves would continue their noise until daybreak.

The lands belonging to the Negro brotherhood of Olinda were very conveniently situated for Jaguaribe, and for another plantation not far distant, which was owned by an old man of color, who harbored around him a numerous clan of relations and dependents. It was arranged that we should rent these lands equally; but to prevent competition, one of us only was to apply for them, and then they were to be divided. The owner of the plantation in question was to make the application, and I rested satisfied; but I was surprised to discover, that I run much risk of remaining without any part of them; therefore I began to make arrangements for obtaining them for myself. While the matter was yet in doubt, a person who was under the protection of the rival plantation sent a number of Negroes to work upon some land which lay very near to Jaguaribe. I sent a message to the owner of these men, purporting that the land was tenanted by a person of my acquaintance, who yearly rented it from the brotherhood, and therefore I requested him to direct that his slaves should retire. This he refused to do; consequently I collected a number of my free workmen, and rode toward the spot in question. The matter had become serious, and as he was aware that if a scuffle ensued, he might lose the service of a slave, while I who was accompanied by free men would not sustain any loss, he gave the desired directions, and I returned home.

I gained my object of renting the lands through the interest of some persons who were intimately acquainted with the principal officers of the brotherhood. I attended at the council table of these black directors, and heard the arguments for and against the policy of placing the whole of the property in the hands of one person; however the matter was decided as soon as one of them rose up and reminded the rest that the community was in debt, and that the new tenant was prepared with one year's rent in advance. All objection was silenced by this speech, and the papers were signed without any further remark. The black gentlemen came down to Jaguaribe to put me in possession of the lands. I had invited several of my friends on this occasion, and blacks and whites all sat down and ate together; the health of our Lady of the Rosary was drunk first; then that of the chief of the brotherhood and of the new tenant. These fellows amused us much, for their politeness to each other, and to the white persons who were present sat awkwardly upon them but was displayed to show the importance which they imagined themselves to possess. The *juiz* or chief of the brotherhood was a shoemaker at Olinda, and the rest were of the same rank in life, more or less.

Possession was given to me, and everything unpleasant seemed to have subsided when one night late a mulatto man, who resided at Jaguaribe, knocked at my door and told me that he had just arrived from a visit to a neighboring cottage, and that on the way three men had come out upon him, and had commanded him to stop; but on seeing him alone, they had retreated. I had had some intimation of what I was to expect, and immediately supposed by whom these persons must have been sent, and for whom the blow was intended. I called two Indians and my faithful slave Manoel, and accompanied by these and the mulatto man who had given me the information, I set off toward the spot. They were gone—but we pursued; however, before we reached the nearest plantation, we heard the heavy gate of its field shut to; therefore it was useless to proceed farther, for the persons, whosoever they were, had reached a place of safety. Upon this path resided the families of the neighborhood with whom I was the most intimate, and it was well known that I sometimes returned home at a late hour. This was a turbulent district in which I had fixed my residence. Some of the owners of the plantations around were perpetually squabbling, and I had been led into the same way of proceeding; indeed, if I had not done so, I should have been trampled upon. The slaves of Paulistas and of Timbó were constantly at war, and the owners of the plantations of Timbó and Jenipapeiro were likewise with law suits always pending, and their dependents never easy. Some districts are in a quieter state than others, but very few are totally without disturbance; and there are few plantations in any part of the province about the boundaries of the lands of which more than one law suit has not been entered into.

I was often reminded by many of my new acquaintances that every plantation ought to have a chaplain; and I was told that without a doubt all those persons who attended to hear mass would contribute toward the payment of the priest, as is customary. I spoke to a young man of this profession for the purpose, and he attended every Sunday and holiday; but when he was dismissed, at the time I was preparing to leave the place, I was left to pay him entirely myself; everyone was poor and unable to assist when the day of payment came. This was only what I expected; but I thought it was right to follow the usual custom of having mass said regularly, on account of the slaves.

In April I arranged with the tenant of the lands which lie to the eastward of Jaguaribe, and are called Maranguape, to allow me to turn loose upon them all my cattle during the rainy season, for the field of the plantation was not sufficiently large to support so great a number of animals, during the whole year, as the work which was performed upon it required. The lands upon which I intended the cattle to remain are about one league in length, and of about half the breadth. Part of them are under water in the rainy season, and in other places they were covered with woods; but these were, for the most part to be entered even on horseback, owing to the cattle feeding in them, and beating down the brushwood. It was astonishing to see in how short a period the cattle which had been accustomed to labor became wild and comparatively fierce. I was in the habit of going occasionally with another person, both of us being on horseback, to collect the animals for the purpose of seeing that none were missing; we had many hard chases after them, and got many blows from the branches of the trees, etc.

A short time after the cattle had been at Maranguape, I agreed with an Indian to go and stay there, for the purpose of taking care of them. This man was in my debt for clothing, and for a gold chain which he had given to his wife. He came to me a few days after his removal, asking leave to go to his former place of residence, which was at some distance, and to take his family with him. I understood what this meant; he would never have returned, and therefore I answered that he might go if he thought proper, but must leave some pledge for the payment of the debt. This he promised to do. Julio, who had been with me on my journey to Ceará, was again in my service. He now displeased me exceedingly, for he too, led astray by this fellow, wished to leave me; Julio had been accused of some petty thefts, with which I now taxed him; he denied having committed them, and that he was innocent I verily believe. However I did not think so then, consequently this circumstance, and his wish to leave me with a man whom I knew to be very unprincipled, for I had lately had information respecting him from other quarters; and above all, the suspicion that they had come at an hour when few persons were about me, under the impression that being alone I should be induced to accede to their demands, caused us to part on bad terms. They went their way toward Maranguape, and I had some hopes that all would have continued quiet. However in the afternoon, about half an hour before the close of the day, the manager came to tell me that Francisco José, the Indian who was in my debt, had passed through the field, accompanied by his wife, Julio, and a number of other Indians. Thus he had determined to go in defiance of any right which I might have to his services, or to demand payment of what he owed me, and in breach of promise given to me only a few hours before. Several other laborers were also indebted to me, and if this man was, without remark, permitted to make his own terms, I knew not who might choose to do likewise.

My horse was brought out; I beckoned to Manoel, my constant companion, and calling to some freemen who had returned from their work, and were now talking together in a group; I said, "Who follows me?" On arrival at the gate of Jaguaribe, I was informed that the party had quartered itself in a corner of the field, in and about the hut of another Indian; to this place we now directed our steps. Francisco José himself came out to speak to me, and soon several others placed themselves near to him. I sat on horseback, holding a parley, my men being on the other side of me, until Antonio, the mulatto carrier, (he who had been waylaid a long time before) came round and leaned against the horse's neck, placing himself between me and the Indian. I afterwards found out, that he had observed that Francisco José held a drawn knife, and Antonio judged that this was intended against me or my horse, for the Indian well knew that if he wounded me, it would probably enable him to escape. Several persons belonging to the plantation had now joined us, and the matter ended by the Indian allowing himself to be taken without resistance, and to be put into the stocks; a party of mulattos, or of creole Negroes, would not have submitted thus quietly. Late at night he paid the debt, was released, and I saw no more of him for a considerable time.

I was now dismissing all those workmen who were not in debt to me, and at last only a few persons remained whose services I required, and upon whose character I could depend. It was very seldom that I visited Recife; but when there was a necessity for so doing, I took advantage of moonlight nights in preference to travelling in the daytime, and was on these occasions accompanied by Manoel.

Several months now succeeded each other without any disquietude. I had another attack of ague during the rainy season, which was, however, much less violent than that of the preceding year. I likewise met with an accident which had nearly proved fatal, occasioned by a blow from the fore feet of a horse; he reared and struck me.

I had had some intention of leaving Jaguaribe, owing to the turbulence of the neighborhood, to my ill health, and to some disagreeable occurrences which had taken place between my landlord and myself. However, as this would have been very inconvenient, I resolved to stay, notwithstanding all these and other disadvantages.

Preparations were made in the month of August for setting the mill to work; the cane had not attained this year its accustomed growth in most parts of the country, and that which I possessed was particularly stunted in size, for I had not commenced planting until it was almost too late. Everything being ready toward the end of the month, I sent for a priest to bless the works. Unless this ceremony is performed, every person who is to be employed about the mill, both freeman and slave, would be afraid to proceed to his destined labor; and if any accident happened, it would be ascribed to the wrath of heaven for this breach of religious observance. The priest arrived and

said mass, after which we breakfasted and then proceeded
to the mill. The manager and several other freemen and
the Negroes stood around the works; a quantity of cane
was placed ready to be thrust in between the rollers, and
the four Negroes whose part it was to feed the mill stood at
their posts. Two lighted candles were placed close to the
rollers, upon the platform which sustains the cane, and a
small image of our Saviour upon the cross stood between
them; the priest took his breviary and read several
prayers, and at stated places, with a small bunch of weeds
prepared for the occasion, which he dipped in a jug of holy
water, he sprinkled the mill and the persons present. Some
of the Negroes sprang forward to receive a good quantum
of this sanctified water; and then the master of the sugar
boiling-house led the way to the portion of the works of
which he had the direction; and here there was another
sprinkling. When we returned to the part of the mill in
which the rollers stood, the priest took a large cane, and I
did the same; then the signal being given, the floodgate
was opened, and the works were soon in motion, and according to rule the two canes which the priest and I held
in our hands were the first to be ground. I had heard much
of this ceremony from persons of the country, and I cannot
avoid saying that although something of the ridiculous
may by many persons be attached to it, still I could not
help feeling much respect for it. The excitement of devout
feelings among the slaves, even of those feelings which are
produced by the Roman Catholic religion, cannot fail to
be serviceable; and if men are to exist as slaves, this is
doubtless the religion which is the best adapted to persons
in a state of subjection. Slavery and superstition are, however, two evils which, when combined, are surely sufficient
to cause the misery of any country.

The carts, the oxen and their drivers had not received the priest's benediction; they arrived some time
afterward, bringing loads of canes, and the carts were
ornamented with the longest that could be picked out
placed as flagstaffs, and bearing upon them handkerchiefs

and ribbons. Each cart in succession stood before the door of the dwelling house, and the priest complied with the wishes of the drivers.

There was an old creole Negro residing in the neighborhood of Jaguaribe, whose disposition led him to explore all the woods for miles around in search of game; he preferred this manner of obtaining subsistence to that of daily labor with the hoe or bill hook. He was acquainted with the situations in which the best timber was to be found; and could, in many instances, name the exact spot upon which some particular tree stood, which was required for any given purpose. This man often came to Jaguaribe, and on these occasions I usually called him into the house to hear his stories, while I sat in my hammock smoking. He was fond of tales of ghosts and *mandingueiros*. The latter are famous, among other feats, for handling poisonous snakes, and can, according to his account and that of many other persons, by peculiar noises or tunes, call these reptiles from their holes, and make them assemble around them. These sorcerers profess to render innoxious the bites of snakes to persons who submit to their charms and ceremonies. One of the modes which is adopted for this purpose is that of allowing a tame snake to crawl over the head, face and shoulders of the person who is to be *curado de cobras*, cured of snakes, as they term it. The owner of the snake repeats a number of words during the operation, of which the meaning, if they contain any, is only known to the initiated. The rattlesnake is said to be, above all other species, the most susceptible of attention to the tunes of the *mandingueiros*. The above accounts I should not have related upon the authority of one or two persons. I have heard them repeated by several individuals, and even some men of education have spoken of the reputed efficacy of the tame snakes of the *mandingueiros*, as if they were somewhat staggered in their disbelief of it; the reputation of the *contas verdes* is firmly established in the faith of those persons of the lower ranks who have heard of them. These men certainly do play strange tricks very dexterously.

I had not been so much inconvenienced by snakes as I had imagined I should; I had seen several different kinds in going through the woods, and particularly in that which leads from Jaguaribe to Paulistas. The path through it is not much frequented, and therefore the snakes have become bolder, crossing the road, or running up a bank as I passed along. One afternoon I had a visit with which I could have well dispensed. I happened to look up while sitting in my hammock and saw one of these reptiles, lying quite still upon the top of the wall of the room, in the opening which is formed by the supporters of the roof that rest upon it. I seized a pike and ran it into the snake, thus rivetting it to one of the beams of the roof, while I called to some person to assist me in killing it; but its writhing was so violent that it soon liberated itself and fell from the wall on the outside, where several persons waited for it.

Charms are often supposed to destroy the venom of snakes, and to produce, consequently, the recovery of the person who has been bitten by one of these reptiles. Oil is sometimes used as a remedy, being given in considerable quantities, which are increased or diminished according to the quality of the oil. Rum is likewise administered so as to produce intoxication. I have also seen a small plant, which is known under the name of *hera cobreira*; wherever I have seen it, the plant has been carefully preserved in a pot. The leaves and the softer branches are bruised and are applied to the wound, and the juice which is extracted from them, when mixed with rum or water, is drunk by the patient. I do not vouch for its success; but its name must, I should imagine, have been acquired by its reputation.

The mill was yet at work in September, when the owner of the place applied to me to leave it, as it was convenient to him to come down from another plantation of which he was the owner, and reside at Jaguaribe, from its vicinity to Recife. I agreed to this, but did not wish that he should move until I was about to leave Jaguaribe. However, one morning, a young man who was related to, and employed by him, came to my house, and told me that by order from his kinsman he had (accompanied by a gang of Negroes) taken possession during the night of the cottage which was situated upon the shelf of the hill. I expressed my surprise at his conduct, and said a good deal upon the subject. He, of course, returned for answer that he had only acted according to the orders which he had received. The principal objection which I had to this premature removal arose from the general turbulent character of the slaves of this man, and from the frequency of quarrels between the dependents of those persons whose dwellings were so near to each other as ours had now become.

Several extremely disagreeable occurrences took place, as I had feared would be the case, before I could conveniently remove. Suffice it to say, that I made a visit to the owner of the plantation of Amparo, in the island of Itamaracá, upon whose lands I agreed to plant sugar canes, and to share with him their produce, as is a usual practice upon sugar estates.

In the beginning of November, 1813, I sent my manager to prepare a residence for me at the town of Conception in the island; and I moved to that place in the course of the following month.

XI

Life on Itamaracá

The island of Itamaracá, which is in length about three leagues, and in breadth about two, is situated at the distance of eight leagues to the northward of Recife, and is entirely separated from the main land by a channel of unequal width, varying from one league to half a mile. The island does not contain any stream of water, but in the neighborhood of the town water gushes from the hill wherever it is dug for. That which is obtained from the springs in the neighborhood of Pilar is not, however, good. Itamaracá is, perhaps, the most populous part of the province of Pernambuco, taken as a whole, the immediate vicinity of Recife excepted. It contains three sugar mills, which are well stocked with Negroes; and many free persons likewise reside upon the lands belonging to them. Besides the lands attached to these works there are other considerable tracts which are subdivided among and owned by a great number of persons of small property. The shores of the island are planted with coconut trees, among which are thickly scattered the straw cottages of fishermen; and oftentimes are to be seen respectable whitewashed dwellings, which are possessed by persons whose way of life is frugal, and yet easy. The salt works upon the island are likewise one great source of its wealth; these are formed upon the sands which are overflowed by the tide at high water.

The long village of Pilar, situated upon the eastern side of the island, is at the present day the principal settlement, although that which is called the town of Conception, where I now resided, standing upon the SE side of the island, claims seniority; but its better times are gone by.

I happened to arrive at Conception upon the day of the festival, the 8th of December. However, as I had many matters to arrange, I did not see the ceremony in the church, but was invited to dine with the vicar. I went at two o'clock, and found a large party assembled, to which I was happy in being introduced, as it consisted of several priests who are the men of most information in the country, and of some of the first laymen of the island. The dinner was excellent and elegant, and the behavior of the persons present was gentlemanly. I was placed at the head of the table, being a stranger; and a friend of the vicar took the opposite end of it, while he himself sat on one side of me. I never met a pleasanter dinner-party; there was much rational conversation and much mirth, but no noise and confusion. The company continued together until a late hour, and indeed the major part of the priests were staying in the house.

The parish of Itamaracá has now for some years enjoyed the blessings which proceeded from the appointment of the present vicar, Pedro de Souza Tenorio. His merit was discovered by the governor, whom he served as chaplain, and by whose application to the Prince Regent was obtained for him his present situation. The zeal of the vicar, for the improvement of the districts over which he has control, is unremitted; he takes pains to explain to the planters the utility of the introduction of new modes of agriculture, new machinery for their sugar mills, and many alterations of the same description which are known to be practiced with success in the colonies of other nations; but it is not every novelty which meets with his approbation. It is no easy task to loosen the deep-rooted prejudices of many of the planters. He is affable to the lower ranks of people, and I have had many opportunities of hearing persuasion and entreaty made use of to many of his parishioners, that they would reform their habits. His occasional extempore discourses on subjects of morality, when seated within the railings of the principal chapel, delivered in a distinct and deep-toned voice, by a man of commanding person, habited in the black gown which is usually worn by men of his profession, were very impressive. He has exerted himself greatly to increase the civilization of the higher orders of people in his parish; to prevent feuds among them; to persuade them to give up those notions of the connection between the patron and the dependent, which are yet too general; he urges them to educate their children, to have their dwellings in a state of neatness, to dress well themselves, their wives, and their children. He is a good man; one who reflects upon his duties, and who studies to perform them in the best manner possible. He has had the necessity of displaying likewise the intrepidity of his character—his firmness as a priest, his courage as a man—and he has not been found wanting. He is a native of Pernambuco, and has not degenerated from the high character of his provincial countrymen; he was educated at the university of Coimbra in Portugal.

From the state of society and government in Brazil, the individual character of the person who holds any office of importance makes a most wonderful difference, and indeed in some districts a man of an active mind with some wealth, but without any appointment, has more weight than a person of a contrary disposition, although the situation of the latter might give him great power, if he thought proper to exert himself.

I passed some portion of each day with the vicar and his party; the conversation never flagged, and I often thought how very superior the persons were with whom I associated, to any that my friends in England could suppose a country residence in Brazil to afford. I was myself agreeably surprised at the change which I had made from Jaguaribe.

I was much surprised at the manner in which even the people of color dress themselves to go to mass in all the villages; if the family is in a respectable way of life, the younger females wear on these occasions gowns of printed cottons, English straw bonnets, stockings also of foreign manufacture and neat shoes which are made by workmen of the country. The young men appear in nankeen pantaloons, and jackets of printed cottons, shirts of cambric muslin, hats of English make, stockings and shoes. Indeed, of late years, since articles of dress have been cheap, and have come into general use—since emulation has arisen, and the means of showing it has been afforded, every hamlet sends forth its rival belles and beaux.

I frequently visited the plantation of Amparo, which is conducted in the manner which I had attempted at Jaguaribe; but here it was performed with more system. The owner of this place employed constantly great numbers of free workmen of all castes; but the Indians formed the principal part of them, and as their master, I suppose, finds it impossible to keep them under due control, the disturbances which are raised upon the estate, and which are entered into at other places by his men, are very numerous. But this person would have done much service to the country in general, if he had managed to keep them in due order, for in that case he would have proved the possibility of the introduction of free men as daily laborers, without the opinion of their unruliness being unavoidable having been adopted by great numbers of the planters.

In the month of January, 1814, the vicar summoned me to accompany him to Pilar, which is distant from Conception two leagues. This village is composed of several irregular streets, formed of small houses of various descriptions; they are constructed of brick, of mud and of coconut leaves. It is a place of some trade, and is likewise frequented by the small craft which sail between Recife and Goiana. The inhabitants support themselves by their fisheries, by the hire of their *jangadas* and canoes, and lately, by the preparation of the outward husk of the coconut for the manufacture of cordage, which has been recently established in the vicinity of Recife. The fishery of Pilar is of considerable importance. The largest portion of the fish which is caught upon this and the adjacent coast, is obtained by means of pens that are generally constructed near low watermark.

In March took place the yearly festival of our Lady of the Rosary, which was directed by Negroes; and at this period is chosen the King of the Congo nation, if the person who holds this situation has died in the course of the year, has from any cause resigned, or has been displaced by his subjects. The Congo Negroes are permitted to elect a king and queen from among the individuals of their own nation; the personages who are fixed upon may either actually be slaves, or they may be manumitted Negroes. These sovereigns exercise a species of mock jurisdiction over their subjects which is much laughed at by the whites; but their chief power and superiority over their countrymen is shown on the day of the festival. The Negroes of their nation, however, pay much respect to them. The man who had acted as their king in Itamaracá (for each district has its king) for several years was about to resign from old age, and a new chief was to be chosen; he who had been fixed upon for this purpose was an old man and a slave, belonging to the plantation of Amparo. The former queen would not resign, but still continued at her post. The old Negro who was this day to be crowned, came early in the morning to pay his respects to the vicar, who said to him in a jocular manner, "Well, sir, so to-day I am to wait upon you, and to be your chaplain." About eleven o'clock I proceeded to the church with the vicar. We were standing at the door when there appeared a number of male and female Negroes in cotton dresses of colors and of white, with flags flying and drums beating; and as they approached we discovered among them the king and queen and the secretary of state. Each of the former wore upon their heads a crown, which was partly covered with gilt paper and painted of various colors. The king was dressed in an old-fashioned suit of divers tints, green, red, and yellow; coat, waistcoat, and breeches; his scepter which was of wood, and finely gilt, was in his hand. The queen was in a blue silk gown, also of ancient make; and the wretched secretary had to boast of as many colors as his master, but his dress had evident appearances of each portion having been borrowed from a different quarter, for some parts were too tight and others too wide for him.

The expense of the church service was to be provided for by the Negroes; and there stood in the body of the church a small table, at which sat the treasurer of this black fraternity (*irmandade*), and some other officers, and upon it stood a box to receive the money. This was produced but slowly, much too slowly for the appetite of the vicar, who had not breakfasted, though it was now nearly midday, for he and his assistant priests were to chant high mass. Therefore he approached the table and began to expostulate with these directors, declaring that he would not go to the altar until every expense was paid. I was much amused to see him surrounded by the blacks and abusing them for their want of punctuality in their contributions. There was soon an uproar in the church among the Negroes; the vicar had blamed some of them, and now, when he left them to themselves, they called each other to account, and the consequences were that many high and angry words passed between them in the church. It was a most entertaining scene to me and a few other persons who stood by and heard what was going on. However, at last Their Majesties knelt down at the railing of the principal chapel and the service commenced. As soon as this was over, the new king was to be installed; but as the vicar was hungry, he dispatched the matter without much ceremony; he asked for the crown, then went to the church-door. The new sovereign presented himself and was requested or rather desired to kneel down; the insignia were given to him and the vicar then said, "Now, sir king, go about thy business."

After my removal in April to the Toque, for so my new dwelling was called, I led a life of quietude; and to one who has not known other countries, and does not feel that a residence in Brazil is a species of banishment, it would be a life of great happiness. I went out young, and therefore had few unpleasant feelings of this kind to conquer, but when I reflect upon the line of life in which I had taken my station, I am happy that I was removed. The climate, in particular, fascinates everyone; the heat is scarcely ever disagreeable, and the power of the sun is rendered less perceptible by the freshness of the sea breeze; the coolness of the night, too, removes all lassitude, if any should have been felt. I have often sat at my door when the moon has been so clear as to render reading by her light, though somewhat irksome, still not difficult. When the night has been dark, I have watched the lights which were to be seen upon the sandbanks, that proceed from the land on each side of the entrance of the harbor; they were frequented at low water by numbers of persons in search of shellfish. The appearance was singular, for the lights seemed to float upon the water.

The first business of the morning was to see that the people went out to work at the proper time; then the stable and other matters of the same kind were to be attended to; for in everything which is to be done by slaves, the master or his deputy must keep his eye as much upon what is going forward as possible. After this I breakfasted, and then either read or wrote, or mounted my horse and rode to the spot upon which my people were at work. I dined about two o'clock, and afterward sat in my hammock smoking; any of the secondary people, or of those in the lower ranks of life, would sometimes about three or four o'clock come to speak to me upon business, or to ask or communicate news, and so forth. Soon after four o'clock, I usually rode out again to see the work, and returned about five or half past. The remainder of the daylight was often expended in reading, and at times the vicar or someone else would come and sit with me until seven o'clock. Sunset in retired situations usually produces melancholy feelings, and not less unpleasant was this period under the circumstances in which I was placed. The Negroes were coming home straggling from their work, fatigued and dirty; the church bell tolled dismally at intervals, that all Catholics should count their beads; the sea looked black, and the foliage of the trees became rapidly darker and darker as the sun sank behind the hills. There is scarcely any twilight in those regions; the light is in a few minutes changed into darkness, unless the moon has risen. Her light is not afforded gradually, but her power is perceived very shortly after the setting of the sun. In the evening I sat and smoked in the open air, and if it was at the time of spring tides, I had a fire made to windward, on account of the mosquitos, and of a very diminutive species of black fly, of which the bite is as painful as that of the mosquito. If these tormentors were too troublesome to be endured, or if I was so inclined, I would close my door and window, and read or write until ten or eleven o'clock, and then go to bed.

Two boys, resident at Conception, were sent to Recife for the purpose of being inoculated with the cowpox; as soon as they returned, the surgeon of Igaraçu, a young man of considerable merit who had been educated at Lisbon, came over to the island to inoculate any persons who might be inclined to undergo the operation. Among the children it was almost general. Their parents and friends were told that the disorder was not infectious, and consequently no precautions were taken in separating those who were under its influence from the other inmates of the same cottage. Soon afterwards an elderly woman, the attendant of a child who had been inoculated, fell sick and died, and other persons were likewise afflicted with the same disorder. The infection spread, and ten or twelve persons died of it in the island. The evil indeed was only stopped by the inoculation of great numbers of the inhabitants. It was observed that none of the individuals who had been inoculated had been in danger, and therefore it was soon seen that the wisest plan was to undergo the operation. A few, however, were so much alarmed at the fate of some of their acquaintances, that they lived for many days in the woods, scarcely visiting any habitation of man in the dread of infection. It was proved that the smallpox did not exist at that time upon the island, for every inquiry was made, much pains were taken by many persons of zeal and activity to certify that this was the case; and indeed when that dreadful malady appears in any neighborhood, the whole country round is alarmed and

every precaution is taken to prevent communication.
Now, it was generally said that either the boys who had
been sent to Recife were inoculated with the smallpox instead of the cowpox, or that the cowpox degenerated and
became an infectious disease. The boys received the matter from a newly-imported Negro, who had, it is true, been
inoculated with the cowpox, but he might have had the
smallpox upon him at the time, though it had not made its
appearance. It is from the newly-arrived Africans that the
smallpox is often spread abroad, after the country has had
a long respite from this much dreaded disorder. One man
who resided near Conception caught the disease and died;
he had only sat for a short time in an outward room of a
house, in the interior of which some children were confined who had been inoculated.

The unfortunate result of this trial of the new disorder rivetted many persons in their prejudices against it;
and others who had strenuously recommended its adop-
tion began to stagger and to fear that they had been de-
ceived. However, as none of those who were inoculated
had been in danger, the people did not appear to have
taken a thorough dislike to it. To me this was a most
anxious time; my establishment of slaves and free people
consisted of twenty-five persons, of whom scarcely any had
had the smallpox. They were too many to inoculate at
once, and therefore I cut off all communication with my
neighbors. This was done without much difficulty;
Manoel was armed, and was ready to prevent any one
from approaching the place, and this I could do without
injustice, for the path led only to the house. I had several
fierce dogs, which were all let loose on this occasion,
notice being given to the neighborhood of such a measure
having been adopted.

XII

OF ANIMALS AND TREES

The lands of the Engenho Velho were much infested by the red ants; but indeed scarcely any part of the island of Itamaracá is free from those most noxious insects. They are of a dusky red color, and vary from one quarter of an inch to one inch in length. Their bite is painful and they will sometimes fix themselves so firmly with their antennae as to leave their points of them in the wound which they have made. Their food is entirely vegetable. I found them extremely troublesome during the continuance of the rains. They would often make their way between the bricks of the floor of my house, and pick up any particles of flour or any grains of maize which might chance to be strewn upon it.

One evening they made their appearance in such great numbers as to darken the floor of the corner of the room from which they proceeded. I sent for some dried leaves of the coconut tree, and only got rid of the enemy by making a bonfire upon the spot of which they had taken possession.

There is another method of destroying the ants, which has only of late years been introduced, but this is more particularly adapted to their destruction when they are undermining a building. A mixture of brimstone and of any other substances which create a considerable degree of smoke is burnt at the entrance of the anthill, a hole being in the first place dug around it, that the combustible matter may be laid rather lower than the surface of the ground immediately surrounding. Then a large pair of bellows is made use of to blow the smoke down the aperture; now all the crevices by which the smoke is again ejected should be stopped up.

The red ant is particularly destructive to the manioc

plant, and in many parts it is almost impossible to preserve the plantations of it from them.

The house in which I resided at Jaguaribe, had been in former times a barn in which the sugar was put into chests for exportation; and I had heard from the neighbors that the ants about it were numerous and particularly a small black ant called the *formiga louca*, or foolish ant, owing to its not appearing to have any track, but to wander about the spot upon which the horde has appeared, running fast to and fro, and irregularly. One evening I had been asleep in my hammock, and was not a little surprised on waking to see that part of the wall opposite to me, which was whitewashed, appeared to be covered with a piece of black cloth; I got up and approached it with the lamp in my hand. I soon saw what it was, and could not help shuddering, for the sight, I may say, was horrible; myriads of these ants were marching along the wall, and their numbers were rapidly increasing. I had scarcely recovered from the first surprise, when on looking round, I saw that the other side of the room was in the same state; I left the place quickly, and calling to some of the Negroes, desired them to bring coconut and palm leaves in abundance. This was done, and operations being actively set on foot against them by applying lighted leaves to the walls, we soon got rid of the major part of the ants.

The ants were not my only persecutors at Itamaracá, for these were assisted by the *cupim* (*termes arborum*), who build their enormous nests, called in Brazil *panelas* (pots), among the rafters of houses, which they destroy in the course of time; and likewise they form their settlements upon trees. They oftentimes made their covered ways along the whitewashed walls of my house, or up the door posts; but I took every precaution against them, which was more particularly necessary in this instance, as my dwelling was not built of the best kinds of timber. I was advised to besmear the places in which they persisted in attempting to build with treacle, and I found that this was successful in making them alter their proceedings. It is well known in that country by all those persons who have paid any attention to the subject that there are certain kinds of timber which are more liable to be attacked by these insects than others.

I have not yet mentioned all the persecutors; for besides those which have been here named, and the famous *chiguas*, there are the *moribundos*, a black insect. The *moribundo* is supplied with wings and has a most painful sting in the tail. It forms its nest upon the trunks and branches of trees; and in clearing lands, the Negroes always proceed with much care, that they may not be taken unawares by these insects; for on a nest being disturbed, they fly out in great numbers. Notwithstanding every precaution, this will occasionally happen; and I have known a Negro to be unable to work for several days after he has been stung by them. The parts which are affected swell and become inflamed, and the sufferer experiences for a day or two the alternate sensations of violent cold and burning heat, similar to the symptoms of aguish disorders.

The bats also annoyed me, for they persecuted my horses. They fasten upon the ears of the beasts, or upon their backs, if there is any spot from which the skin has been rubbed. The skin of an owl is often hung up in a stable for the purpose of scaring the bats.

The island of Itamaracá is said to be less infested with snakes than the mainland, and perhaps this opinion is founded on experience; but some of those which are generally accounted venomous certainly exist upon it. The most beautiful reptile which I saw was the *cobra de coral*, or coral snake or worm. It is about two feet in length, and of the thickness of a man's thumb; it is marked with black, white and red stripes transversally. The general opinion is that it is venomous.

But the snakes do not cause so much annoyance as the smaller species of vermin which I am about to mention, because the former seldom enter the houses, nor are they very frequently to be seen in the paths or roads. But the *aranha caranguejeira*, or crab-spider (*aranea avicularia*), the *lacraia*, or scorpion, and the *piolho de cobra*, or snake-louse (*scolopendra morsitans*) are to be met with in the houses and in all situations. They should be carefully avoided, for their bites are painful, and are said to cause inflammation. An instinctive recollection of the chance of meeting with these or other vermin of less importance became so habitual with me (and indeed is so with most persons) that when I was about to begin to read, I closed the book in the first place violently so as to crush any thing that might have crept in between the leaves. When my hat or boots or clothes were put on some precaution was taken, as a thing of course. This was not done from a direct idea of the likelihood of finding anything unpleasant in that immediate instance; but the precaution was entered into from habit, unconsciously.

In the month of September I went up the river in a canoe to Igaraçu. The distance from my residence was two leagues.

The mangroves entirely destroy the beauty which it is natural to suppose that the rivers of the country would possess. Until they are destroyed a dull sameness presents itself, for the eye cannot pentrate beyond them. The mangroves grow as far down as low watermark; and when the tide is out, their entangled roots and sprouts, and their stems covered with oysters and besmeared with mud, are left uncovered; but at the height of the tide these are concealed and the water reaches up to the branches of the trees, so that those which bend downward are partly wetted, presenting to the beholder the view of a forest growing in the water. This species of mangrove sometimes attains the diameter of fifteen or eighteen inches, and the height of twenty-five or thirty feet. There are two species with which I am acquainted, the *mangue vermelho* or red mangrove, of which I have been speaking, and the *mangue bravo* or wild mangrove. The bark of the former is used for tanning; and the timber is much esteemed for beams and rafters in building; but it cannot be used as posts, for under ground it decays very quickly, nor as railings, for it does not bear exposure to the weather.

As I did not, in 1814, suppose that on the following

year I should be recalled, I began to make some addition to my cottage, for it was too small for me; and besides it was old and was constructed of bad timber, which caused it to be much infested by the ants and the *cupim*. The *pão ferro*, or iron wood, which is also called the *coração de negro* or the Negro's heart, was the most valuable of those which I employed. The outward coat of the wood of this tree is not particularly hard, but the heart destroys many hatchets. I have seen some of this timber taken out of the ground, after standing for many years as a support to the roof of a house; and though the outward coat was crumbling into dust, the black heart seemed to be literally of iron, or to have increased rather than decreased in hardness. This wood admits of considerable polish; but the black wood which is most esteemed for furniture is the *jacaranda*. This is also hard, but is much more penetrable than the *pão ferro*, and the polish to which it may be brought is more complete.

The *pão d'arco* is another valuable wood, and is so called, I imagine, from the use which the Indians made of it for their bows; it is much used in building, and is accounted almost as durable as the *pão ferro*. The number of fine species of timber in Brazil is very great, but I am myself acquainted only with a few of them.

I was obliged in September to forsake my house for three days, from a most unexpected cause. A whale was stranded upon one of the sandbanks at the mouth of the harbor, this being the third time that the inhabitants of Itamaracá had been favored with visitors of this description. *Jangadas* were sent out to it; and when the tide came in, it floated and was towed into the harbor, where the persons who were employed in the business landed it, as near as they could at high watermark, in front of and distant from my house about three hundred yards. Many of my neighbors were occupied in making oil; for anyone who pleased was at liberty to take as much of the blubber as he could make use of; and one man fairly got into the whale and ladled out the fat which was melted by the heat of the sun. When the people left the carcass, either at mid-day or at night, it was attacked by numerous flights of *urubus* and was literally covered by them. The trees round about the spot were occupied by these enormous birds, which were waiting for an opportunity of satisfying their boundless appetites. The *urubu* is nearly twice the size of the common crow of England; it is quite black, except at the point of the beak, which is white, as I have been told, but this I did not observe. Wherever there happens to be the carcass of an animal, these birds assemble shortly after the death of the beast.

The stench proceeding from the whale became in a few days so intolerable as to render a removal necessary, and therefore I applied to an old creole black, a carpenter, to allow me to reside in his cottage, which was neat and clean. To this he agreed, while he went to live with some of his friends.

XIII

Tidbits: *Military, Religious and Social*

In the months of August and September, I was fully employed in planting cane.

About this time were issued orders from the governor for recruiting the regiments of the line. The men who are required are pressed into the service. The orders were forwarded to the *capitães-móres*, who again distributed them to the captains. The directions were on this occasion, and indeed always are, that men of bad character between the ages of sixteen and sixty shall be apprehended and sent to Recife for enlistment; and that every family containing two or more unmarried sons shall give one for the service of the country. But it is on these occasions that tyranny has its full sway, that caprice and pique have their full vent, that the most shameful partiality prevails, that the most intolerable oppression is experienced. In fact now it is that the whole country is seen in arms against itself, and that every means of entrapping each other are used by the nearest neighbors. Revenge, violence, deceit and breach of trust are excited, and instead of suppression, they meet with encouragement.

Petitions were sometimes made to the governor in particular instances of injustice; but these were often of no avail, for the custom is that the recruits should be returned as being fit for service as soon as possible after their arrival at Recife, and their names placed upon the rolls, from which none can be removed without an order from the sovereign, although the provincial governor should be aware of the true state of the case.

A young man of respectability was carried before a certain *capitão-mor*, and the alternative was proposed to him either to marry a young woman whom he had never seen, but who happened to be a burden to those persons under whose care she was placed, or to become a soldier. He of course preferred the latter, was sent to Recife and was obliged to enlist.

For some weeks the whole country appeared to be afflicted with a civil war; parties of armed men were to be seen in all directions, in search of those who had concealed themselves. An individual who was not well known could not stir from his home without a pass from the captain of the district in which he resided, stating him to be a married man, or naming some other cause of exemption. Nor is a man who is liable to be pressed, safe in his own house, for the *tropa*, or troop, would surround the cottage in which any of these persons were suspected to have taken refuge, and they would demand admittance. If this was denied, no scruple would be entertained of breaking down the door and entering by force. This occurred to my knowledge in many cases, in several parts of the country. It is among the *Ordenanças* that the recruiting of which I am treating is carried on. Negroes and Indians are excluded from the regiments of the line, the former on the score of color, and the latter from their caste, white men and mulattos of all shades being alone admitted. The great repugnance which is generally felt toward the service is occasioned by the smallness of the pay, and by the want of proper clothing, while the almost incessant duty precludes any hope of working at a trade, or of pursuing any employment that is not connected with the life of a soldier.

The soldier of South America ought to be a being of far different stamp from the soldier of Europe. Any war which it might be necessary for Brazil to wage against a foreign invader should (indeed must) be carried on with a direct view to the peculiar advantages of the country; it would be a *guerrilla* war, a war under the cover of woods and hills. Therefore, although it may be as well to have a few disciplined soldiers who may be preserved, for the purpose of forming the basis of a large force, if circumstances should require it, still it is not by discipline that success will be ensured. It is through the affection which the soldiers feel for their government and for their country that the result will be propitious, or the contrary. If the soldier and the peasant can be combined usefully in the same person, it is in Brazil that such a system should be followed.

I was in the habit of conversing with several of the people of color who resided in my neighborhood. One man particularly amused me much; he was a short and stout creole black, a shoemaker by trade. I was greatly entertained with his pompous manner, exalting in terms of extravagant praise the advantages which Itamaracá enjoyed, and the excellencies of Conception, which was his native spot, in particular. He lamented much the removal of the mayor and chamber to Goiana, giving me to understand that undue influence had been employed, forgetful of the insignificance of one place and the importance of the other. He also told me with much vehemence of voice and action that the late vicar had wished to remove the image of our Lady of Conception from the parish church to Pilar; but that the inhabitants assembled and prevented the accomplishment of the plan. "No," he said, "if that image was to leave us, we should consider ourselves unprotected, and then indeed would our town be utterly destroyed." The vicar of whom the man spoke might have gone to reside at Pilar if he pleased, but *he*, too, had his prejudices in favor of the image, and did not like to say mass before any other in his own parish. Thus images cease to be regarded as the representations of those to whom prayer is to be addressed; a value is placed upon the wood itself, and religion degenerates into unveiled idolatry.

The sexton of the parish church, who was a mulatto man, had much peculiarity of character. He had a great deal of penetration, but was extremely cautious in what he said; and when questions were asked relating to any affair in which he thought he might become implicated, he usually answered—"Where white men are concerned, Negroes must be silent." This fellow was once holding a candle in the hand of a dying person, and repeating the word "Jesus," as is customary; the patient began to move restlessly but Gonsalo quietly went on with his dismal work and added with perfect unconcern, "Come die, and have done with your nonsense."

The creole Negro of whom I have above spoken was fond of shooting the larger kinds of game, such as antelopes, which are called in the country *veados* and *pacas*. This was done in the following manner:—A platform of thick twigs was made among the branches of a tree, at the height of several feet from the ground, near to some one of those plants upon whose leaves or fruit these animals feed. At night two men placed themselves upon this platform, and when the footsteps of the animal were heard, one of the men would light a small taper prepared for the occasion, and the other, with his gun ready, looked round for the game. The animal was allowed to come as near as it seemed inclined to do unmolested, and was then fired at. The men immediately descended, and oftentimes did not attempt to find their prey until the morning; returning to the spot for the purpose. This is the usual manner of obtaining these animals.

I heard accidentally, in conversing with persons of the lower ranks in life, of an instance in which the Indians continued their heathenish customs. A family resided at a plantation in this neighborhood, which had much intimacy with many Indians, but none of the members of it were of that caste. When the heads of the families were from home, the young females were in the habit of meeting to amuse themselves. On one of these occasions, an Indian girl carried one of her companions into the hut in which she and her parents dwelt, and on this playmate questioning her, from girlish curiosity, about several gourds which were hanging up in the room, she appeared much alarmed, and said, "You must not look that way, those are *maracás*, which my father and mother generally put into their chest, but they have to-day forgotten them." Notwithstanding her entreaties to the contrary, her companion took hold of one of the gourds, and moving it quickly discovered that there were pebbles within. They had handles to them, and tufts of hair upon the top, and they were cut and carved in divers unusual forms. Here this matter ended, but soon afterwards several of the mulatto women agreed to watch the Indians, for they knew that they often danced in their huts with closed doors. This was an uncommon practice, and inconvenient too, for the open air is much pleasanter. They had soon an opportunity of witnessing one of these meetings. The huts are constructed of coconut leaves, and through these they managed to obtain a view of what was going forward. There was a large earthen pot in the center; and round this both men and women were dancing. A pipe was handed occasionally from one to the other. Soon afterwards one of the Indian girls told one of her companions of a different caste from her own, as a great secret, that she had been sent to sleep at a neighbor's hut a few nights before because her father and mother were going to drink *jurema*. This beverage is obtained from a common herb; but I never could persuade any of the Indians to point it out to me; though when they positively asserted that they were unacquainted with it, their countenances belied their words.

I had a visit in October from a strange old man whose age was generally supposed to border upon ninety years. He was a creole black, and had been a slave upon the plantation of Santos Cosmo e Damiam in the várzea to the southward of Recife; he had settled at Igaraçu after he obtained his manumission, having married, when he was about seventy years of age, a young woman of his own color; and he was now surrounded by a young family. This man did not reckon his age by years, but by the governors; and as each of these, with few exceptions, remained at the head of the province only three years, something near the truth could be collected. This mode of computation is very common. I have often, on asking the age of any person, received for answer, that the individual concerning whom the inquiry was made had been born in the first, second or third year of such a governor. The dreadful famine of 1793 is also an era from which the peasants date many circumstances.

Some of my neighbors, both at Itamaracá and at Jaguaribe, chanced at times to come in while I was reading, and would be curious to know how it was that I could find amusement in being so employed. I remember one man saying to me, "You are not a priest, and therefore why do you read; is that a breviary in which you are reading?" On another occasion, I was told that I had got the character among the people of color in the neighborhood of being very holy, for I was always reading. A person who can read, write and keep accounts has attained the height of perfection, and is much respected; or rather of late years, one who does not know how to do these things is looked down upon. The women particularly pride themselves upon the superiority which they enjoy by this means; by which they are brought to an equality with their husbands. In the above general character of the free people, I do not include the planters of large property, for their acquirements are oftentimes considerable. The Indians, too, are quite separate, owing to their degraded state. However I include the white persons of small property. It is surprising, though extremely pleasing, to see how little difference is made between a white man, a mulatto and a creole Negro if all are equally poor and if all have been born free. I say surprising, because in the English, French and Dutch colonies the distinction is so decidedly marked; and among the Spaniards, lines are even struck between the several shades of color.

One day the old man [Apollinario] came to me with a face of dismay, to show me a ball of leaves tied up with *cipó*, which he had found under a couple of boards upon which he slept in an outhouse; for he had removed from the house of his friend in the town to my place. The ball of leaves was about the size of an apple. I could not imagine what had caused his alarm, until he said that it was *mandinga*, which had been set for the purpose of killing him; and he bitterly bewailed his fate, that at his age anyone should wish to hasten his death and to carry him from this world before our Lady thought fit to send for him. I knew that two of the black women were at variance; and suspicion fell upon one of them who was acquainted with the old _mandingueiro_ of Engenho Velho, therefore she was sent for. I judged that the _mandinga_ was not set for Apollinario, but for the negress whose business it was to sweep the outhouse. I threatened to confine the suspected woman at Pilar, and then to send her to Pará, unless she disclosed the whole affair; this she did, after she heard me tell the manager to prepare to take her to Pilar. She said that the _mandinga_ was placed there to make one of the Negroes dislike her fellow-slave and prefer her to the other. The ball of _mandinga_ was formed of five or six kinds of leaves of trees, among which was the pomegranate leaf. There were likewise two or three bits of rag, earth of a peculiar kind, ashes which were of the bones of some animal; and there might be other ingredients besides, but these were what I could recognize. The woman either could not from ignorance, or would not, give any information respecting the several things of which the ball was composed. I made this serious matter of the _mandinga_, from knowing the faith which not only many of the Negroes have in it, but also some of the mulatto people. However I explained to everyone that I was angry with her from the bad intention of the scheme, and not from any belief that it would have any effect. There is another name for this kind of charm; it is _feitiço_, and the initiated are called _feiticeiros_.

I was invited about this period to attend the funeral of a young married woman of respectable family. I went about five o'clock to the house of the vicar, that I might go with him and three other priests. From hence we adjourned at dusk to the church, where the priests, all of whom were already in their black gowns, put on over these the short lace rochet, and the vicar took in his hands a large silver cross. We walked to the house in which the body was laid; this was habited in the coarse brown cloth of the Franciscan order, for the deceased had belonged to the lay sisterhood of the Third Order of St. Francis; the face was uncovered, and the body was laid upon a bier, the room being lighted with many torches. The habits in which the bodies of the deceased lay brothers and sisters of the Third Order are dressed are obtained from the convents of St. Francis, and are said to be the habits of deceased friars; but probably the worn-out dresses of those who still live are likewise sold, and thus arises a considerable source of revenue to the convent. There were assembled in the room several of her male relations and others who had been invited. After a good deal of chanting, a wax taper was given to each person present, and these being lighted, we proceeded to the church which was hard-by, walking in pairs; the bier followed, carried by four persons, and there was chanting as we went along. In the middle of the body of the church, a scaffolding was erected of about four feet from the ground, and upon this the bier was placed, the attendants standing round while the priests chanted. The body was soon put into the grave which was in the church, and there was lime in it. The friends of persons deceased aim at having as many priests at the funeral as they can collect and afford to pay; though on the occasion of which I speak, the priests served without any remuneration, for the young woman was the near relative of a priest with whom the others were intimate. Likewise all the neighbors who are of an equal rank with the deceased are invited to attend, that the ceremony may be as splendid as possible. Notwithstanding the manifest inconvenience, and the mischief which the unwholesomeness of the custom might, and perhaps does cause, all bodies are buried within the churches. Indeed the prejudice against being buried in the open air is so great that even the priests would not dare to alter this mode of proceeding, supposing that they wished so to do.

Toward the end of the same month (November), it is customary for the vicar to determine upon those persons who are to sustain the expenses of the nine evenings previous to the festival of Our Lady of Conception—that is, to

supply the bonfires, gunpowder, oil, etc. Each evening is
provided for on all these occasions, by one or more persons
of the immediate neighborhood, and a greater or less expense is incurred, according to the means and the inclination of the individuals who have been named. It was my
general practice to accompany the vicar to church on
Sundays and holidays, returning with him to his house to
breakfast. I was in the church when he read over the list of
the names of those who were to provide for the nine evenings, and was somewhat surprised to hear my own in con-
junction with that of a neighbor, for the ninth night. I had,
however, some suspicion that this would be the case, for I
had heard some whisperings upon the subject among the
secondary people; the custom is to keep the individuals
who are to be concerned ignorant of what is intended. We
began on the following morning to make preparations for
the occasion, and sent to Recife for the colors of several
ships, some gunpowder, fireworks, and a few of the musicians of the band of the Olinda regiment, applying through
a friend for the consent of their colonel. We likewise sent
for Nicolau, a creole black and a tailor by trade, whose
merry tongue and feet made him like dancing and singing
better than the needle; and we agreed with him to bring
over from the village of Pasmado, a set of *fandango* performers. The colors were raised upon long staffs, very
early in the morning of our day, in two rows along the area
of the town. As the sun rose, several guns were fired—of
those which are usually made use of at festivals; they are
composed of a small and short iron tube which has a
touch-hole of disproportionate dimensions; they are placed
upright upon the ground, and the match is then applied.
In the course of the day the band played, and in the evening were kindled about twenty bonfires in the square of
the village. The houses were illuminated with lamps,
which were made of the half of the rind of an orange, each
containing a small quantity of oil and cotton. There were
likewise great numbers of large crosses, lighted up in the
same manner in several parts of the square. The church

was crowded, and the noise of the people was great; the guns were fired at intervals; the musicians of the festival, with violins and violoncellos, played within the church, and the Olinda men on the outside; and rockets were let off occasionally: Indeed the confusion was extreme. Some of the numerous horses which stood in all quarters, tied to railings or to door-posts, or held by little children, while their masters were amusing themselves, took fright and broke loose, adding not a little to the noise and bustle. All the affairs in and about the church ended at so late an hour that the *fandangos* were deferred until the following evening. The band had been playing close to the door of the vicar's residence, which was much crowded with several of the first families of the island; and in the front of the house a great concourse of people was assembled. At the moment that the music ceased, an *improvisador* or *glosador*, as these persons are there called, delivered a few verses in praise of the vicar; he then praised Our Lady in a strange style, giving her every fine epithet, whether appropriate or not, which came to his recollection. Then he rang changes upon every body he could think of, and I heard the name of Henrique da Costa, to which mine was metamorphosed, thrown in every now and then among the rest. I was praised for my superior piety, in giving so splendid a night in honor of Our Lady. On the following morning every arrangement was made for the *fandangos*. A spacious platform was erected in the middle of the town and in front of the vicar's dwelling, raised about three feet from the ground. In the evening four bonfires were lighted, two being on each side of the stage, and soon afterwards the performers made their appearance. The story which forms the basis of this amusement is invariably the same; the parts, however, are not written, and are to be supplied by the actors; but these, from practice, know more or less what they are to say. The scene is a ship at sea, which, during part of the time is sailing regularly and gently along; but in the latter part of the voyage she is in distress. The cause of the badness of the weather remains for a long time unknown; but at last the persons who are on board discover that it has arisen from the devil, who is in the ship, under the disguise of the mizzen-topmastman.

Twelve men and boys, who are dancers and singers, stand on the stage, six of them being on each side of it; and the leader of the chorus sits at the back of the stage with a guitar, with which he keeps the time, and this person is sometimes assisted by a second guitar player. A ship is made for the occasion; and when the performers stepped on to the platform, the vessel appeared at a distance under full sail, coming toward us upon wheels, which were concealed. As soon as the ship arrived near the stage, it stopped, and the performance commenced. The men and boys who were to sing and to dance, were dressed in white jackets and trousers; they had ribbons tied round their ankles and arms, and upon their heads they wore long paper caps, painted various colors. The guitar player commenced with one of the favorite airs of the country, and the chorus followed him, dancing at the same time. The number of voices being considerable, and the evening extremely calm, the open air was rather advantageous. The scene was striking, for the bonfires threw sufficient light to allow our seeing the performers distinctly; but all beyond was dark, and they seemed to be enclosed by a spacious dome. The crowd of persons who were near the stage was great, and as the fires were stirred and the flame became brighter, more persons were seen beyond on every side; and at intervals the horses, which were standing still farther off, waiting for their masters.

When the chorus retired, the captain and other superior officers came forward, and a long and serious conversation ensued upon the state of the ship and the weather. These actors were dressed in old uniforms of the irregular troops of the country. They were succeeded by the boatswain and the two clowns; the former gave his orders, to which the two latter made so many objections that the officer was provoked to strike one of them, and much coarse wit passed between the three. Soon afterwards came the chaplain in his gown, his breviary in his hand; and he was as much the butt of the clowns as they were of the rest of the performers. The most scurrilous language was used by them to him; he was abused, and was taxed with almost every irregularity possible. The jokes became at last so very indecent as to make the vicar order his doors to be shut. The dancers came on at each change of scene. I went home soon after the vicar's doors were closed, and did not see the conclusion; but the matter ended by throwing the devil overboard and reaching the port in safety. The performers do not expect payment, but rather consider themselves complimented in being sent for. They were tradesmen of several descriptions residing at Pasmado, and they attend on these occasions to act the *fandangos*, if requested so to do; but if not, many of them would most probably go to enjoy any other sport which the festival might afford. We paid their expenses, and gave them their food during their stay; they were accompanied by their families, which were all treated in the same manner, to the number of about forty persons.

I was invited in January 1815 to attend a christening at the sugar plantation of Macaxeira, which is the largest and most valuable in every respect of the three in the island. As soon as the christening was over, the day was devoted to eating and drinking and playing at cards. When the men had left the table after dinner, the cloth was again laid, and the ladies sat down to dine; but one of the priests declared that this separation was barbarous, and seating himself again, was followed by several other men. Thus they dined a second time. The evening ended rather boisterously, but good-humoredly; the wine was poured out into tumblers, and these being as frequently emptied as if they had been smaller, only a few of the guests returned home the same night; but those who remained crept off early and quietly on the following morning.

I accompanied the vicar to Pilar to pass the *entrudo* at that place. We set off on the Saturday afternoon. On the following day, after the service of the church was over, the *entrudo* jokes and tricks began, and before the conclusion of the sport in the evening, each person had been obliged to change his clothes several times. The ladies joined with heart and soul, and particularly the good old lady of Macaxeira, who was wet through and through, and yet carried on the war. The priests were as riotous as the rest, but their superiority of manner even here was perceivable; their jokes were well-timed, and were not accompanied by any brutality of behavior; there was a seeming deference in their manner when they were drenching the person upon whom they made an attack; and they took care that what they threw was clean, which with others did not always happen.

On Monday morning everyone rose fresh for action, and to work we went until three o'clock in the afternoon, scarcely affording time for eating. We then adjourned to the seashore, for the purpose of witnessing the christening of the king of the Moors. On this day all the *jangadas* and canoes were put in requisition; the owners of them and others of the inhabitants of the neighborhood were divided into two parties, Christians and Moors. A stage was erected at low watermark upon high poles, and this was intended to represent a Moorish fortress; the affair was so timed that the tide should be at the height at the commencement of the sport, by which means the stage was surrounded by the water. Upon the seashore were two high thrones, with canopies made of counterpanes, etc. These were at the distance of about three hundred yards from each other, and were placed immediately above high watermark. The Christian king sat upon one of them, and the Moorish king upon the other, both of them being habited in fine flowing robes. The affair began by the former dispatching one of his officers on horseback to the latter, requiring him to undergo the ceremony of baptism, which he refused to do. Several other couriers passed from each side, all of whom were on horseback, and fantastically dressed in loose garments. War being declared, the numerous *jangadas* and canoes of each party were soon in motion, making toward the fortress in the water; some were going to assist in protecting it, and others to obtain possession of it. The persons who were in the fort were now seen preparing for its defence; there was much firing, and at last, after many struggles on both sides, it was taken by the Christians. The Moorish vessels, however, escaped and landed their crews, the opposite party doing the same. The armies met on shore and fought hand to hand for a considerable time, but in the end the Moorish king was taken prisoner, hurled from his throne, and forcibly baptized. The whole affair was very gay, for the sands were crowded with people who were all in their best clothes, finery of many kinds being displayed—silks, satins, muslins, and printed cottons; ornaments of gold and of precious stones; bonnets of straw, and of silks, and ribbons of all colors in great quantities; shoes, white, black, and of various tints; then there were coats that had not for many a day seen the light; cotton and cloth jackets made for the occasion, embroidered waistcoats, and others more general of less costly materials; pantaloons of nankeen and of various other light materials; cocked hats, a few of beaver and of straw, and round ones many; half boots, and shoes and buckles.

Shortly after this period I received advices from England which rendered necessary my return home. I gave up my plan of residing in Brazil with reluctance; but I am now much rejoiced that it so happened. Yet at that time it required some resolution to leave the people, the place, and the things in which I had taken deep interest—my Negroes and free people, my horses and my dogs, and even my cats and fowls, the house and the garden which I had been improving and forming, and the fields which I had cleared and was cultivating. All this, believe me, cost much pain in leaving. England is my country, but my native soil is Portugal; I belong to both, and whether in the company of Englishmen, of Portuguese, or of Brazilians, I feel equally among my countrymen.

XIV

AGRICULTURE: *Sugar, Cotton, Manioc and Coconuts*

The lands in Brazil are never grubbed up, either for planting the sugar cane, or for any other agricultural purpose. The cane is planted among the numerous stumps of trees, by which means much ground is lost, and as the sprouts from these stumps almost immediately spring forth (such is the rapidity of vegetation), the cleanings are rendered very laborious. These shoots require to be cut down, sometimes even before the cane has forced its way to the surface of the ground. The labor likewise is great every time a piece of land is to be put under cultivation, for the wood must be cut down afresh; and although it cannot have reached the same size which the original timber had attained, still, as several years are allowed to pass between each period at which the ground is planted, the trees are generally of considerable thickness. The wood is suffered to remain upon the land until the leaves become dry; then it is set on fire, and these are destroyed with the brushwood and the smaller branches of the trees. Heaps are now made of the remaining timber, which is likewise burnt. This process is universally practiced in preparing land for the cultivation of any plant. I have observed that the canes which grew upon the spots where the heaps of timber and large branches of trees have been burnt, were of a darker and richer green than those around them, and that they likewise over-topped them. After the plant-canes or those of the first year's growth are taken from the lands, the field-trash, that is the dried leaves and stems of the canes which remain upon the ground, are set fire to, with the idea that the ratoons, that is, the sprouts from the old roots of the canes, spring forth with more luxuriance and attain a greater size by means of this practice. The ratoons of the first year are called in Brazil *socas*; those of the second year,

161

resocas; those of the third year, *terceiras socas*, and so forth. After the roots are left unencumbered by burning the field-trash, the mould is raised round about them; indeed if this was neglected, many of these roots would remain too much exposed to the heat of the sun, and would not continue to vegetate. Some lands will continue to give ratoons for five or even seven years; but an average may be made at one crop of good ratoons fit for grinding, another of inferior ratoons for planting or for making molasses to be used in the stillhouse, and a third which affords but a trifling profit, in return for the trouble which the cleanings give.

I have above spoken more particularly of high lands; the low and marshy grounds, called in Brazil *várzeas*, are however those which are the best adapted to the cane, and indeed upon the plantations that do not possess some portion of this description of soil the crops are very unequal, and sometimes almost entirely fail, according to the greater or less quantity of rain which may chance to fall in the course of the year. The *várzeas* are usually covered with short and close brushwood, and as these admit, from their rank nature, of frequent cultivation, they soon become easy to work. The soil of these, when it is new, receives the name of *paul*; it trembles under the pressure of the feet, and easily admits of a pointed stick being thrust into it; and though dry to appearance, it requires draining. It is, I believe, generally acknowledged that no land can be too rich for the growth of the sugar cane. One disadvantage, however, attends soil that is low and quite new, which is that the canes run up to a great height without sufficient thickness.

The general mode of preparing the land for the cane is by holing it with hoes. The Negroes stand in a row, and each man strikes his hoe into the ground immediately before him, and forms a trench of five or six inches in depth; he than falls back, the whole row doing the same, and they continue this operation from one side of the cleared land to the other, or from the top of a hill to the bottom. The earth which is thrown out of the trench remains on the lower side of it.

The plough is sometimes used in low lands, upon which draining has not been found necessary; but such is the clumsy construction of the machine of which they make use that six oxen are yoked to it. Upon high lands the stumps of the trees almost preclude the possibility of thus relieving the laborers.

The trenches being prepared, the cuttings are laid longitudinally in the bottom of them, and are covered with the greatest part of the mould which had been taken out of the trench. The shoots begin to rise above the surface of the ground in the course of twelve or fourteen days. The canes undergo three cleanings from the weeds and the sprouts proceeding from the stumps of the trees; and when the land is poor, and produces a greater quantity of the former and contains fewer of the latter, the canes require to be cleaned a fourth time. It is often judged proper to thin the canes by removing some of the suckers at the time that the last cleaning is given, and some persons recommend that a portion of the dry leaves should also be stripped off at the same period, but on other plantations this is not practiced.

The proper season for planting is from the middle of July to the middle of September, upon high lands and from September to the middle of November in low lands. Occasionally the great moisture of the soil induces the planter to continue his work until the beginning of December, if his people are sufficiently numerous to answer all the necessary purposes. The first of the canes are ready to be cut for the mill in September of the following year, and the top is finished usually in January or February.

There is also a strange custom among the lower orders of people; they scruple not in passing a field, to cut down and make a bundle of ten or a dozen canes, from which they suck the juice as they go along, or preserve some of them to carry home. The devastation which is committed in this manner is incalculable, in the fields that border upon much frequented paths. It is a custom; and many persons think that the owner has scarcely a right to prevent these attacks upon his property.

The planters of Brazil have not yet arrived at the period (which is not however far distant) of being under the necessity of manuring their lands. I heard of very few instances in which this is the practice.

A sugar plantation is doubtless one of the most difficult species of property to manage in a proper manner. The numerous persons employed upon it, their divers avocations, and the continual change of occupation, give to the owner or his manager constant motives for exertion, innumerable opportunities of displaying his activity. A plantation ought to possess within itself all the tradesmen which are required for the proper furtherance of its concerns: a carpenter, a blacksmith, a mason, a potter, and others which it is needless to name. It is a manufactory as well as a farm, and both these united must act in unison with each other, and with the seasons of the year.

The mill ought, properly, to commence grinding the cane in September, but few of them begin until the middle of October; for the planting scarcely allows that they should set to work before the latter period. This is the time of merriment and of willing exertion, and for some weeks the Negroes are all life and spirit; but the continuance of constant work for the whole of the day and part of the night at last fatigues them, and they become heavy and fall asleep wherever they chance to lay their heads.

The mills for grinding the canes are formed of three upright rollers. Two men and two women are employed in feeding the mill with cane; a bundle of it is thrust in between the middle roller and one of the side rollers, and being received by one of the women, she passes it to the man who stands close to her, for the purpose of being by him thrust between the other side roller and that of the center. This operation is continued five or six times until the juice has been extracted. The Negroes who thrust the cane in between the rollers have sometimes allowed their hands to go too far, and one or both of them having been caught, in some instances, before assistance could be given, the whole limb and even the body has been crushed to pieces. In the mills belonging to owners who pay attention to the safety of their Negroes, and whose wish it is to have everything in proper order, a bar of iron and a hammer are placed close to the rollers upon that table (*mesa*) which supports the cane. The bar is intended to be violently inserted between the rollers in case of accident, so as to open them, and thus set at liberty the unfortunate Negro. In some instances I have seen lying by the side of the bar and hammer a well-tempered hatchet, for the purpose of severing the limb from the body, if judged necessary. On these unfortunate occasions, the screams of the Negro have the effect of urging the horses which draw the mill, to run with increased velocity. I am acquainted with two or three individuals who now work their mills with oxen; and they gave as the principal reason for this change, the decrease of danger to the Negroes who feed the mill; because such is the slowness of these animals, that an accident of the above description can scarcely happen, and indeed they are stopped rather than urged to proceed by noise. Some of the mills are turned by water, but many more would admit of this improvement than take advantage of it. Most of the mills are worked by horses. Oxen are usually employed in drawing the carts.

In the boiling-house, the production of sugar in Brazil requires great alteration. The work is done in a slovenly manner, very little attention being paid to the minutiæ of the business. The ovens over which the boilers are placed are rudely made, and they answer the purpose for which they are intended in an imperfect manner. Enormous quantities of fuel are consumed, and the Negroes who attend to the ovens are soon worn out. The juice runs from the cane as it is squeezed between the rollers into a wooden trough below, and is from thence conveyed into a cistern made of the same material, standing in the boiling-house. It is received from this cistern into the great caldron, as it is called, which is a large iron or copper vessel. The caldron has previously been heated, and when nearly full, the *temper* is thrown into it, and the liquor is suffered to boil. It is now scummed with considerable labor. The work of scumming is usually performed by free persons, which is owing to two causes: it demands considerable skill, to which slaves seldom attain; and the exertion which it requires induces the planter to pay a free man, rather than injure one of his own people.

From the first caldron or clarifier, the liquor is ladled out into a long trough or cistern, which is generally made of the trunk of one tree; and in this it remains until it becomes tepid. The labor which the operation of ladling requires is excessive, the heat and smoke of a boiling-house in a tropical climate increasing greatly the violence of the exertion. From this trough, which holds the whole of the contents of the great caldron, the liquor when sufficiently cool is suffered to run into the first copper, and from this it is removed into a second and a third copper, and some boiling-houses contain a fourth. From this it is ladled into large jars, called *formas*, when the master of the boiling-house judges from the touch that the syrup has arrived at a proper consistence. The jars are afterwards taken into the adjoining building, in which the sugar is to undergo the process of claying. The sugar, after being clayed, is invariably dried in the sun.

The *temper* which is usually made use of is the ashes of wood calcinated, of which there are certain species preferred for this purpose. There exists a general prejudice against lime, under the idea that the sugar with which it has been made is unwholesome; and this has prevented many persons from adopting it.

The Brazil planters are more backward in the management of their stillhouses than in any other department of their business. The stills are earthen jars with small necks, and likewise small at the bottom, widening upwards considerably, but again straightening on approaching the neck. The foundation of a circular oven is formed, and two of these jars are placed within it, one on each side of it, in a slanting position, with the bottom within the oven and the neck on the outside, and being thus secured the walls of the oven are built up against them, and the top is closed in. These stills have round caps, *carapuças*, which fit on to the mouths of the jars, and are rendered perfectly tight by a coat of clay being daubed round the edges, after the *wash* has been put into the still and the fire has been lighted underneath. These caps have on one side a pipe of six inches in length attached to each of them, and into this is inserted the end of a brass tube of four feet in length. This tube is placed in a broad and deep earthen pot or jar containing cold water, and the opposite end of it reaches beyond the pot. The tube is fixed with a sufficient slant to allow of the liquor running freely through it. The liquor which is obtained from the first distillation is usually sold, without undergoing any further process. A second distillation is only practiced in preparing a small quantity for the use of the planter's house.

The property of sugar planters, which is directly applied to the improvement, or to the usual work of their plantations, is not subject to be seized for debt; this privilege was granted for the encouragement of the formation of such establishments, but it may have a contrary effect. The planter is allowed many means of evading the demands of his creditors, and everything is permitted to act in his favor.

Most of the plantations of the first class are however in the hands of wealthy persons, and this is becoming more and more the case every day. The estates which may be said to constitute this class are those which are situated near to the seacoast, that is, from two to sixteen miles from it; which possess a considerable portion of low land adapted to the planting of the sugar cane—another of virgin wood—good pasture-land, (for nature must do every thing,) and the possibility of being worked by water.

The lands of sugar plantations are appropriated to five purposes. These are: the woods, the lands for planting canes, those which are cleared for pasturage, the provision-grounds for the Negroes, and the lands which are occupied by free people.

The buildings which are usually to be seen upon the plantations are the following:

The mill, which is either turned by water or by cattle; some of the plantations possess both of these, owing to the failure of the water in the dry season; and indeed there are a few estates upon which the crops are so large as to require that there should be both.

The boiling-house, which is usually attached to the mill, and is the most costly part of the apparatus for the coppers, etc. must be obtained from Europe.

The claying-house or *caza de purgar*, which is often-times connected with the boiling-house. It is also generally made use of as the stillhouse or distillery.

The chapel, which is usually of considerable dimen-sions. This building and all the foregoing are almost uni-versally constructed of brick.

The dwelling house for the owner or manager; to this is usually attached a stable for the saddle horses; the dwell-ing houses are frequently made of timber and mud.

The row of Negro dwellings, looking like neglected almhouses in England, is made of the same materials as the house of the owner. From the appearance of the Negro huts an idea may usually be formed of the disposition of the owner of a plantation. All these buildings are covered with tiles.

The estates have no regular hospital for the sick Ne-groes; but one of the houses of the row is oftentimes set apart for this purpose. The stocks, in which disorderly slaves are placed, stand in the claying-house.

An estate which possesses forty able Negroes, males and females, an equal number of oxen, and the same of horses, can be very well worked; and if the lands are good, that is, if there is a fair proportion of low and high lands fit for the culture of the sugar cane, such an estate ought to produce a number of chests of sugar, of fifteen hundred weight each, equal to that of the able slaves. I speak of forty slaves being sufficient, because some descriptions of work are oftentimes performed by freemen; thus, for instance, the sugar-boilers, the person who clays the sugar, the distiller, the cartmen, and even some others, are very frequently free.

The Negroes may be valued at 32*l*. each; oxen at 3*l*. each; and horses at the same; but by management the two last may be obtained at lower prices. A sugar plantation of the first class, with suitable buildings, may be reckoned as being worth from £7000 to £8000, and some few are valued as high as £10,000. The inland plantations may be reckoned at from £3000 to £5000 and a few are rather higher. Plantations of the first class ought to have eighty Negroes at least, and an increased number of animals, owing to their capability of employing more hands.

The only carts which are used upon the plantations are very clumsily made; a flat surface or table (*mesa*) made of thick and heavy timber, of about two feet and a half broad, and six feet in length, is fixed upon two wheels of solid timber, with a moveable axletree; a pole is likewise fixed to the cart. These vehicles are always drawn by four oxen or more, and as they are narrow, and the roads upon which they must travel are bad, they are continually overturning.

COTTON

This most valuable plant has now become of more importance to Pernambuco even than the sugar cane, owing to the great demand for the cotton of that province, and of those adjoining to it, in the British markets. The districts which are chosen for the purpose, and universally allowed to be the best adapted to its growth, are far removed from the seacoast, arid, and oftentimes very scantily supplied with fresh water. The cotton plantations are yearly receding farther into the interior, wherever the sertão plains do not prevent this recession. The cotton is often sold by the planter in *caroço*, that is, before it has been separated from the seed, to other persons whose livelihood is obtained in preparing it for the export market; but as the labor of conveyance is, of course, considerably increased while it is in this state, the dealers establish themselves near to the plantations; they recede as the planters recede. Some years ago a number of the machines for separating the cotton from the seed were to be seen within two leagues of Recife; a few years after they were removed to Goiana, and now the principal resorts of the dealers are Limoeiro and Bom Jardim; places, as will have been seen, which are several leagues distant from the coast.

The lands are cleared for planting cotton in the usual manner—by cutting down the trees and burning them; and the holes for the seeds are dug in quadrangular form at the distance of six feet from each other. Three seeds are usually put into each hole. The time for planting is in January after the *primeiras águas* or first waters; or at any rate as soon in the year as any rain has fallen. Maize is usually planted among the cotton shrubs. Three crops and sometimes four are obtained from the same plants; but the second crop is that which generally produces the finest wool.

The profits which are obtained in favorable years by the planters of cotton are enormous; but frequently disappointments are experienced. Oftentimes a whole crop is totally lost, and instead of large returns, the year proves entirely unproductive; or after a fair promise, the grub, the caterpillar, the rain, or the excessive drought destroys all hope until the following season. The other great agricultural object, the sugar cane, is not subject to those numerous and ruinous reverses.

The quality of the cotton which is produced in South America, either to the north or south of Pernambuco, is inferior to that of the province of which I am treating. The cotton of Ceará is not so good, and the cotton of Maranhão is still coarser. Cotton is the staple commodity of both these ports. Proceeding from Pernambuco to the south, the cotton of Baía is not so fine, and the small quantity which is produced at Rio de Janeiro is not so good as that of Baía.

MANIOC

The manioc requires good land, and the same spot will not produce two crops successively; it must be allowed to rest for one or two years or more. The operation of planting it is simple, and differs in no respect from that which was practiced formerly by the Indians. The flour which is made from this root is called *farinha de pão*, or stick-flour. There are several species of the manioc plant, of which some are adapted to high lands, and others to low and moist situations; but when the plant is cultivated upon the latter, hillocks must be raised, else the root would decay. Although the manioc plant requires a dry situation, still when the rains fail in January the crops fall short, for it is in this month, immediately after the first waters, that the principal plantations of it are made.

The most expensive part of the process of making the flour of the manioc consists in disengaging the rind from the root. This is done with difficulty, by means of a piece of a broken blunt knife, a sharp pebble, or a small shell, with one of which each person is supplied. In this work a considerable number of persons must be occupied, to furnish employment to the wheel which grinds the root. This wheel is placed in a frame and a handle is fixed to it on each side, by which it may be turned by two men, one of them working at each of the handles. A trough stands under the wheel, and the wheel is cased in copper, which is made rough by means of holes punched in it; the sides of the holes are not filed smooth. The manioc is thrust against the wheel while it is turned with great velocity, and being by this means ground, it falls into the trough underneath. From hence the ground pulp is put into a press, that the juice may be extracted; and after it has undergone sufficient pressure, this pulp or paste (*maça*) is removed to a hot hearth, upon which a person is employed to keep it in continual motion, that it may not be burnt. When quite crisp it is taken off the hearth, and on being suffered to cool is in a state to be made use of.

There is another mode of preparing the manioc for food; it is put into water in a pannier or closed basket, and is allowed to remain there for some days, until the root becomes soft, from which the manioc, when in this state, is called *manioca mole*. It is prepared in this manner for the purpose of making cakes, etc. but not, generally, for food. The smell from the *manioca mole* is extremely offensive, and is one of the annoyances in walking the streets of Recife, in which it is sold. The smell is, however, entirely removed after the *farinha* has been for some minutes upon the oven.

COCONUTS

The sandy soils of the coast in which this plant seems to delight would, if they were not cultivated with it, remain almost useless; but from the produce which the coconut tree yields they are rendered very valuable. The lands which are occupied by this plant alone yield a settled income to the owners of them without much labor; while the cultivation of any other requires considerable toil. However the long period, of from five to seven years, which the tree requires before it bears fruit, cannot fail to be considered a drawback upon the profits which it ultimately affords. It is a most valuable production, of which every part is appropriated to some useful purpose. The Brazilians say that it affords them both food and shelter; of the trunk and of the leaves their huts are built; of its fibrous roots baskets are made, and cordage of the outward husk. Its fruit renders them meat and drink, and an excellent oil is likewise to be obtained by skimming the juice which may be pressed from the pulp. The coconut is in general use in cookery among all ranks of people, and it forms one of the chief articles of internal trade. When a plantation of this tree is about to be established, the ripe coconuts from which the plants are to be reared are placed in the ground, about twelve inches below the surface, in long and almost united rows, for the convenience of being watered. They are frequently placed in this manner under the eaves of houses, which saves much trouble, for by the accumulation of water from the housetop each shower of rain produces sufficient moisture, and the owner is relieved from any farther trouble in this respect. At the expiration of five months the shoots begin to make their appearance above ground, and at the end of twelve months from the time that the coconuts were first put into the earth, the young plants may be removed. They are then placed at the distance of eight or ten yards from each other, upon the land that has been cleared for the purpose of receiving them. As soon as they have once taken root, and by far the major part of them do, very little care is necessary. They must, however, be preserved tolerably free from brushwood, at least during the first years; and indeed at all times the fruitfulness of the tree will be increased, if it is allowed its due space.

XV

PEOPLE: *Free and Slave*

The free population of Brazil at the present time consists of Europeans; Brazilians, that is, white persons born in Brazil; mulattos, that is, the mixed caste between the whites and blacks, and all the varieties into which it can branch; mamalucos, that is, the mixed caste between the whites and Indians, and all its varieties; Indians in a domesticated state, who are called generally caboclos; and those who still remain in a savage state, and are called generally tapuios; Negroes born in Brazil, and manumitted Africans; lastly, mestizos, that is, the mixed caste between the Indians and Negroes.

First we must treat of the whites. The Europeans who are not in office, or who are not military men, are, generally speaking, adventurers who have arrived in that country with little or no capital. They look down upon the Brazilians, or rather they wish to consider themselves superior to them.

I have observed that, generally speaking, Europeans are less indulgent to their slaves than Brazilians. This difference between the two descriptions of owners is easily accounted for; the European has probably purchased part of his slaves on credit, and has during the whole course of his life made the accumulation of riches his chief object. The Brazilian inherits his estate, and as nothing urges him to the necessity of obtaining large profits, he continues the course that has been pointed out to him by the former possessors.

Notwithstanding the relationship of the mulattos on one side to the black race, they consider themselves superior to the mamalucos; they lean to the whites and, from the light in which the Indians are held, pride themselves upon being totally unconnected with them. Still the mu-

lattos are conscious of their connection with men who are
in a state of slavery, and that many persons even of their
own color are under these degraded circumstances; they
have therefore always a feeling of inferiority in the company of white men, if these white men are wealthy and
powerful. This inferiority of rank is not so much felt by
white persons in the lower walks of life, and these are more
easily led to become familiar with individuals of their own
color who are in wealthy circumstances. Still the inferiority which the mulatto feels is more that which is produced
by poverty than that which his color has caused, for he will
be equally respectful to a person of his own caste who may
happen to be rich. In Brazil, even the trifling regulations
which exist against them remain unattended to. A mulatto enters into holy orders or is appointed a magistrate,
his papers stating him to be a white man, but his appearance plainly denoting the contrary. In conversing on one
occasion with a man of color who was in my service, I asked
him if a certain *capitão-mor* was not a mulatto man; he
answered, "he was, but is not now." I begged him to explain, when he added, "Can a *capitão-mor* be a mulatto
man?"

The regiments of militia, which are called mulatto
regiments, are so named from all the officers and men being of mixed caste; nor can white persons be admitted into
them.

Marriages between white men and women of color
are by no means rare, though they are sufficiently so to
cause the circumstance to be mentioned when speaking of
an individual who has connected himself in this manner;
but this is not said with the intent of lowering him in the
estimation of others. Indeed the remark is only made if the
person is a planter of any importance, and the woman is
decidedly of dark color, for even a considerable tinge will
pass for white. If the white man belongs to the lower orders,
the woman is not accounted as being unequal to him in
rank, unless she is nearly black. The European adventurers often marry in this manner, which generally occurs

when the woman has a dower. Still the Brazilians of high birth and large property do not like to intermarry with persons whose mixture of blood is *very* apparent.

The mamalucos are more frequently to be seen in the sertão than upon the coast. They are handsomer than the mulattos; and the women of this caste particularly surpass in beauty all others of the country; they have the brown tint of mulattos, but their features are less blunt, and their hair is not curled. I do not think that the men can be said to possess more courage than the mulattos; but whether from the knowledge which they have of being of free birth and on both sides, or from residing in the interior of the country where government is more loose, they appear to have more independence of character, and to pay less deference to a white man than the mulattos. When women relate any deed of danger that has been surmounted or undertaken, they generally state that the chief actor in it was a large mamaluco, as if they thought this description of men to be superior to all others. Mamalucos may enter into the mulatto regiments, and are pressed into the regiments of the line as being men of color, without any regard to the sources from which their blood proceeds.

I now proceed to mention that numerous and valuable race of men, the creole Negroes—a tree of African growth which has been transplanted, cultivated and much improved by its removal to the New World. The creole Negroes stand alone and unconnected with every other race of men, and this circumstance alone would be sufficient, and indeed contributes much to the effect of uniting them to each other. The mulattos, and all other persons of mixed blood, wish to lean toward the whites, if they can possibly lay any claim to relationship. Even the mestizo tries to pass for a mulatto, and to persuade himself, and others, that his veins contain some portion of white blood, although that with which they are filled proceeds from Indian and Negro sources. Those only who can have no pretensions to a mixture of blood call themselves Negroes, which renders the individuals who do pass under this denomination much attached to each other, from the impossibility of being mistaken for members of any other caste. They are handsome persons, brave, hardy, obedient to the whites, and willing to please; but they are easily affronted, and the least allusion to their color being made by a person of a lighter tint, enrages them to a great degree. They will sometimes say, "A Negro I am, but always upright." They are again distinct from their brethren in slavery, owing to their superior situation as free men.

The free creole Negroes have their exclusive regiments, as well as the mulattos, of which every officer and soldier must be perfectly black.

The creole Negroes of Recife are, generally speaking, mechanics of all descriptions; but they have not yet reached the higher ranks of life, as gentlemen, as planters, and as merchants. Some of them have accumulated considerable sums of money, and possess many slaves. The Negroes are excluded from the priesthood; and from the offices which the mulattos may obtain through their evasion of the law, but which the decided and unequivocal color of the Negro entirely precludes him from aspiring to. In law all persons who are not white, and are born free, class equally; manumitted slaves are placed upon the same footing as persons born free. However, although the few exclusions which exist against the Negroes are degrading, still in some instances they are befriended by them. They escape the persecutions under which the other castes suffer during the time of recruiting.

The men whose occupation it is to apprehend runaway Negroes are, almost without exception, creole blacks; they are called *capitães-do-campo*, captains of the field; and are subject to a *capitão-mor-do-campo* who resides in Recife, and they receive their commissions either from the governor or from this officer. By these they are authorized to apprehend and take to their owners any slaves who may be found absent from their homes without their master's consent. Several of these men are to be found in every district, employing themselves in such pursuits as they think fit, when their services are not required in that calling which forms their particular duty. They are men of undaunted courage, and are usually followed by two or three dogs.

It is scarcely necessary to name the mestizos, for they usually class with the mulattos; nor are they to be easily distinguished from some of the darker varieties of this caste. A dark-colored man of a disagreeable countenance and badly formed person is commonly called a mestizo, without any reference to his origin.

Indian slavery has been for many years abolished in Brazil, and the individuals who are now in bondage in that country are Africans, and their descendants on both sides, or individuals whose mothers are of African origin; and no line is drawn at which the near approach to the color and blood of the whites entitles the child, whose mother is a slave, to freedom. I have seen several persons who were to all appearance of white origin still doomed to slavery.

Slaves, however, in Brazil have many advantages over their brethren in the British colonies. The numerous holidays of which the Catholic religion enjoins the observance give the slave many days of rest or time to work for his own profit; thirty-five of these, and the Sundays besides, allow him to employ much of his time as he pleases. The slave can oblige his master to manumit him, on tendering to him the sum for which he was first purchased, or the price for which he might be sold, if that price is higher than what the slave was worth at the time he was first bought. This regulation, like every one that is framed in favor of slaves, is liable to be evaded, and the master sometimes does refuse to manumit a valuable slave; and no appeal is made by the sufferer, owing to the state of law in that country, which renders it almost impossible for the slave to gain a hearing. Likewise this acquiescence in the injustice of the master proceeds from the dread that if he was not to succeed he would be punished, and that his life might be rendered more miserable than it was before.

A slave is often permitted by his owner to seek a master more to his liking; for this purpose a note is given, declaring that the bearer has leave to enter into the service of anyone, upon the price which the master demands being paid by the purchaser. With this the slave applies to any individual of property whom he may wish to serve.

A considerable number of slaves are manumitted at the death of their masters, and indeed some persons of large property fail not to set at liberty a few of them during their own lifetime. A deed of manumission, however simply it may be drawn out, cannot be set aside. The price of a new-born child is £5 (20,000 *mil-reis*), and the master is obliged to manumit the infant at the baptismal font, on the sum being presented. In this manner a considerable number of persons are set at liberty, for the smallness of the price enables many freemen who have had connections with female slaves to manumit their offspring.

All slaves in Brazil follow the religion of their masters; and notwithstanding the impure state in which the Christian church exists in that country, still such are the beneficent effects of the Christian religion that these, its adopted children, are improved by it to an infinite degree; and the slave who attends to the strict observance of religious ceremonies invariably proves to be a good servant. The Africans who are imported from Angola are baptized in lots before they leave their own shores, and on their arrival in Brazil they are to learn the doctrines of the church, and the duties of the religion into which they have entered. The unbaptized Negro feels that he is considered as an inferior being, and therefore he is desirous of being made equal to his companions.

The slaves have their religious brotherhoods as well as the free persons; and the ambition of a slave very generally aims at being admitted into one of these, and at being made one of the officers and directors of the concerns of the brotherhood. The Portuguese language is spoken by all the slaves, and their own dialects are allowed to lay dormant until they are by many of them quite forgotten. No compulsion is resorted to to make them embrace the habits of their masters, but their ideas are insensibly led to imitate and adopt them. The masters at the same time imbibe some of the customs of their slaves, and thus the superior and his dependent are brought nearer to each other.

The slaves of Brazil are regularly married according to the forms of the Catholic church; the banns are published in the same manner as those of free persons; and I have seen many happy couples (as happy at least as slaves can be) with large families of children rising around them. The masters encourage marriages among their slaves, for it is from these lawful connections that they can expect to increase the number of their creoles. A slave cannot marry without the consent of his master, for the vicar will not publish the banns of marriage without this sanction. It is likewise permitted that slaves should marry free persons; if the woman is in bondage, the children remain in the same state; but if the man is a slave, and she is free, their offspring is also free.

The great proportion of men upon many of the estates, produces, of necessity, most mischievous consequences. If an adequate number of females are placed upon the estate, and the slaves are trained and taught in the manner which is practiced upon well-regulated plantations, the Negroes will be as correct in their behavior as any other body of men.

The slaves who are employed in Recife may be divided into two classes, household slaves and those which pay a weekly stipend to their owners proceeding from the earnings of some employment which does not oblige them to be under the immediate eye of the master. The first class have little chance of gaining their freedom by their own exertions. This second class consists of joiners, shoemakers, canoemen, porters, etc. and these men may acquire a sufficient sum of money to purchase their own freedom.

Creole Negroes and mulattos are generally accounted quicker in learning any trade than the Africans. This superior aptitude to profit by instruction is doubtless produced by their acquaintance from infancy with the manners, customs and language of their masters. From the little experience, however, which I have had, and from the general remarks which I have gathered from others, who might be judged better acquainted than myself with slaves, I think that an African who has become cheerful, and seems to have forgotten his former state, is a more valuable slave than a creole Negro or mulatto.

The newly-imported Negroes are usually sent to work too soon after their arrival upon the estates; if proper care is taken of them, they may indeed be employed in almost any description of labor at the end of eight or ten months, but not much before this period.

There are considerable numbers of white persons and of color who possess two or three slaves, and share with them the daily labor, even of the field. These slaves are, generally speaking, creoles, who have been reared in the family, or they are Africans who have been purchased very young for a trifling sum of money. They are frequently considered as part of the family, and share with the master the food for which both are working. These slaves appear on gala days well dressed, and they have a certain air of independence, which shows that they think themselves to be something more in the world than mere drudges. The difference of the feeling of one of these men toward his master, and that of the generality of the slaves which are owned by great proprietors, is very striking.

From the vastness of the country, it might be supposed that if a slave escapes from his master, the chances would be against his return, but this is not the case. The Africans particularly are generally brought back; they are soon distinguished by their manner of speaking the Portuguese language; and if any one of them cannot give a good account of himself, he will not be allowed to remain long unmolested, for the profit arising from the apprehension of a runaway slave is considerable.

Some of the Negroes who escape determine to shun the haunts of man. They conceal themselves in the woods, instead of attempting to be received into some distant village as free persons. They form huts, which are called *mocambos*, in the most unfrequented spots, and live upon the game and fruit which their places of retreat afford. These persons sometimes assemble to the number of ten or twelve, and then their dislodgment is difficult; for their acquaintance with the woods around gives them the advantage over any party which may be sent to attack them.

That the general character of persons who are in a state of slavery should be amiable, and that goodness should predominate, is not to be expected. We ought rather to be surprised at the existence of that degree of virtue which is to be found among those who are reduced to a situation of so much misery. Slaves are much inclined to pilfer, and particularly toward their masters this is very frequent; indeed many of them scarcely think that they are acting improperly in so doing. Drunkenness is common among them. A direct answer is not easily obtained from a slave, but the information which is required is learnt by means of four or five questions put in various ways. The Negroes show much attachment to their wives and children, to their other relations if they should chance to have any, and to their *malungos* or fellow-passengers from Africa. The respect which is paid to old age is extremely pleasing to witness. Superannuated Africans, upon the estates, are never suffered to want any comforts with which it is in the power of their fellow-slaves to supply them. The old Negroes are addressed by the term of *pai* and *mãe*, father and mother. The masters likewise add this term to the name of their older slaves, when speaking to them. That the generality of the slaves should show great attachment to their masters, is not to be expected; why should they? The connection between the two descriptions of persons is not one of love and harmony, of good producing gratitude, of esteem and respect; it is one of hatred and discord, of distrust and of continual suspicion; one of which the evil is so enormous that if any proper feelings exist in those who are supposed to benefit from it, and in those who suffer under it, they proceed from our nature, and not from the system.